How To Build A Website And Stay Sane

Second Edition

About The Author

Jonathan Oxer is founder and Technical Director of Internet Vision Technologies and is recognized as one of the pioneers of dynamic websites.

Commencing trading in 1994, his business was one of the first in the world to focus on managing commercial website content dynamically using databases. With a rapidly growing reputation and client list it also became one of the first companies ever to do real-time event coverage via the Internet when a live feed was run from the floor of the national Bicycle Industry Trade Show in Sydney, Australia way back in 1995.

Since then Jonathan and his staff have planned, implemented and managed websites, intranets and extranets for companies ranging from tiny backyard businesses to multinational corporations. His clients span many countries, including Australia, Canada, Germany, New Zealand and the United States. You can learn more about Internet Vision Technologies at www.ivt.com.au.

Jonathan is also a Debian GNU/Linux developer and has presented dozens of papers, seminars and tutorials at conferences around the world. He is also a regular guest on radio including the "Byte Into IT" segment on RRR, and he sits on the Advisory Group of Swinburne University's Centre for Collaborative Business Innovation, responsible for researching and developing e-business related curriculum strategies.

He has been a regular contributor to a number of IT magazines including the Australian Linux magazine linmagau with a column titled The Debian Universe, and is author of "Ubuntu Hacks" (O'Reilly, 2006: www.ubuntuhacks.com). His articles and books have been translated into numerous languages including Spanish, Italian, Norwegian, Polish, Brazilian Portuguese, German, and French.

Jonathan also writes an irregular email newsletter called "Jon Oxer's eBusiness News". You can read past editions and subscribe free to receive future updates at www.stay-sane.com/ebusinessnews.

More information about what Jonathan has been up to recently can usually be found on his blog at http://jon.oxer.com.au/.

How To Build A Website And Stay Sane

Second Edition

Jonathan Oxer

First published October 2004 by Oft Press.
Second Edition published May 2007 by Lulu.com.

© Copyright 2004-2007 Jonathan Oxer

ISBN: 978-1-84799-734-0

Disclaimer

This book is sold as is, without warranty of any kind, either express or implied. While every precaution has been taken in the preparation of this book, the author and publisher assume no responsibility for errors or omissions. Neither is any liability assumed for damages resulting from the use of the information or instructions contained herein. It is further stated that the author and publisher are not responsible for any damage or loss to your data or your equipment that results directly or indirectly from your use of this book.

Trademarks

All terms mentioned in this book that are known to be trademarks or service marks have been appropriately capitalized. The author and publisher cannot attest to the accuracy of this information. Use of a term in this book should not be regarded as affecting the validity of any trademark or service mark.

Cover by Rokat Design www.rokatdesign.com.au

*For my father, who never doubted my course
even when sending me emergency food parcels*

*For my mother, who told me that I could do anything
and let me convert her house into an office so I could try*

*For Ann, who took my dreams on as her own
and let me share her dreams too*

*And for Amelia and Thomas,
the greatest blessings a father could have*

ABOUT THIS BOOK

Unfortunately most business operators are woefully unprepared for dealing with a web developer. It's a confusing field with rapidly changing technology, more than a few fly-by-nighters, and many inexperienced "experts". Even dealing with a top-notch development firm can be a painful and frustrating experience if you aren't prepared for the many issues that will crop up along the way, and there are a number of fundamental things that you really should understand when you engage a developer to create or revamp your website.

So after discussing common experiences with other veteran developers as well as many business operators it became obvious that what many people really need is not a technical manual but rather a website development survival guide.

After all, you are giving your developer a great deal of responsibility: how they handle your project will determine the way your organization will interact with the online world. But do you know enough to keep everything on track and understand the decisions your developer will ask you to make?

Imagine someone who has only watched television a couple of times in their entire life. Would they do a good job of hiring a studio to produce TV advertising for their business?

Probably not. They wouldn't be able to make informed decisions, and the studio would probably become very frustrated and blow the project budget just trying to educate them on how to work with the medium.

It sounds crazy but that situation occurs every day with website development projects. The objective of this book is to prevent it happening to you by giving you inside knowledge of the process of site development, the strategic and tactical issues involved, the difficulties you may face and the opportunities that will arise along the way.

THE BOOK SITE

This book has an accompanying website at **www.stay-sane.com**. Things you will find there include links to all the resources referenced throughout this book, making it a convenient jumping off point to investigate Internet project management issues. The site also contains a wealth of tools you may find useful such as a Web Developer Selection Matrix and a Site Critique Form.

The Big Picture

Table Of Contents

Introduction

There is a general feeling in many businesses that they need a website, but they don't really know why or what specific benefit it has for the business. Management hears that "everyone else" has a successful site incorporating the latest online marketing fad, and decides that if they don't have a shiny new corporate website (or intranet, or extranet) up by next Tuesday they must be behind the times. So the CTO, the CIO and the VP of Marketing are hastily called upstairs for an audience with The Man (or The Woman) and charged with making it so. Five minutes later they are standing in the hall, wondering what to do next.

Maybe you're one of them. Maybe you're the one issuing the order. Maybe you're in the position of weighing up the advantages of creating a site in-house versus retaining an external developer. Maybe you're still questioning whether your organization needs a website at all. Maybe you have an existing site in need of an overhaul, and you want to make sure it's done properly. Or maybe you have a site but aren't getting any benefit from it, and you want to know why.

Then this guide is for you.

This guide will **not** try to turn you into a web developer by overloading you with intricate details of Photoshop and HTML and server-side scripting. It **will** get you speaking the same language as your developer and help you avoid many of the problems that leave so many web projects behind schedule and over budget.

As a site owner what you need is an overview of the development process and a structured plan to keep everything on track. What I outline in this book is a 4-phase process used by many professional developers including myself, and you can follow it directly or adapt it to suit your own needs whether you are creating your site in-house or working with an external developer. In my experience the major difference between sites that work and sites that don't is not the technical skill of the developers, it's the process that's followed as the site is created, launched and run. Or more commonly the total lack of a process!

If you'll be producing your site in-house there will be numerous additional technical details for your staff to master, but if you don't get the overall process right it doesn't matter how technically talented your staff are. The end result can still be a dog's breakfast.

Creating a website, intranet or extranet is not a simple job. The process can be long and involved and even if you retain an external developer you need to be committed to doing a lot more than spending five minutes on the phone describing what you want and then waiting to hear that the job is done. As a web developer myself one of the most common (and frustrating) problems I face is clients who underestimate the effort required for a website development project and then run out of steam before it's finished.

Building a site properly involves lots of activities. Imagine how much work it would be to:

- Organize a stand for a trade show
- Design and print new company brochures
- Revise your business plan
- Review your sales procedures
- Redesign and rewrite all your marketing material
- Train new sales staff
- Review and update your entire product database
- Review and possibly rationalize your pricing structure
- Reformat or scan photographs of all your products
- Formalize your customer-support procedure

Now imagine doing them all at the same time, with a deadline.

That's effectively the job that needs to be done, and it will involve both you and your developer taking on different responsibilities at different stages of the action. I don't want to scare you off because most of the hard work should be handled by your developer, but don't start building a commercial website with an unrealistic expectation of the effort involved or the breadth of the issues you will be faced with.

Whether you are developing your site internally or retaining a developer to create a site for you there is a certain minimum level of knowledge you must have in order to avoid a messy meltdown. While seeking input for this book I had conversations with other web developers from around the world, and I asked them all a simple question: "What things do you usually find yourself having to teach new clients?"

Many frustrated developers responded passionately with a list of things they wished all their clients understood. The answers showed great consistency, and the same list was repeated almost verbatim time after time. Visualize your developer on their knees begging you to do each of these things and you'll probably have an accurate picture of the frustration they feel each time they deal with a new client:

- Define project objectives clearly
- Budget time for design reviews
- Supply content on time
- Use appropriate content
- Give thought to promoting the site
- Budget and plan for maintenance and updates
- Don't request inappropriate features just because they're "cool" (chat rooms!)

These issues and many more are covered in this book, giving you the background you need to find a good developer, negotiate a contract, and oversee the process of having your site created or updated. By the time you get to the final chapter you should be able to talk the talk with any web developer on the planet. You'll probably make their day, too, because you'll be one of the most well-informed clients they have the pleasure of dealing with.

The chapters are structured to match the chronological progress of a typical website development project, giving you a good overview of the entire process without forcing you to wade through technical details that are only of interest to your developer. I suggest you read the entire book once through before getting underway, then follow it through chapter by chapter as you have your site developed.

>Getting Started<

Phase 1: Strategic Planning

Phase 2: Design And Engineering

Phase 3: Production

Phase 4: Launch / Promotion

Post-Launch: Running The Site

Endmatter

1. What Can A Website Do Anyway?

Before you jump into a site (re-)development project you need to have some idea what your options are.

I'll start by presenting a few brief case studies, because one of the problems I've seen recently is that too many people are still fixated on creating old-style brochure-ware sites because that's all they're familiar with. Not many industries move faster than Web development so you may not be aware of some of the things that can be done with modern websites, and in particular with dynamic sites – that is, sites that use a database to store content.

As you are about to see, a modern website is a lot more than just a collection of pretty pictures with some text that gets updated every couple of years. These examples will give you an overview of how various organizations have created websites that are timely and useful and usable, not just soon-forgotten money pits.

Keep your own needs in mind as you go through these case studies. Look at the functionality of each example website and imagine it being applied to your business. And try to dream up totally new approaches that I may not have mentioned here, because only you really know your own business.

MOZI

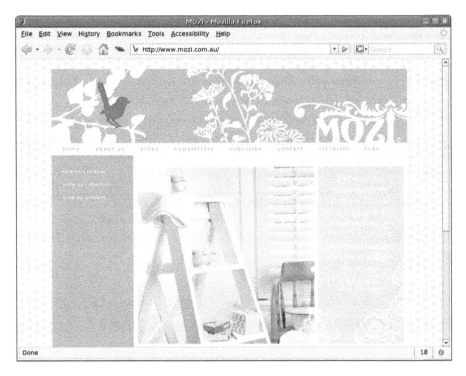

Site: **MOZI**

URL: www.mozi.com.au

I've included MOZI as the first example specifically because it's a typical product-based company. It's exactly the sort of business most likely to fall for the tired old "let's just put our catalog online and forget about it" approach.

Luckily Olivia and Camilla, the business owners, are much smarter than that.

In outward appearance MOZI seems to be a typical retail website and it operates in a way that should be very familiar – you can browse products, place orders, and do all the usual things you'll find on just about any retail site. However, there are some depths to it that may not be immediately obvious.

The first important feature (and you'll soon notice it's a recurring theme throughout this book!) is that the site is "dynamic". We'll get to that in detail later, but basically it means that content you see on the site comes out of a database and can be updated at any time by the site owner. Gone are the days when a site owner needed to call their developer every time they wanted to make a minor change: modern sites let the owner do it themselves in a simple, password-protected area without having to learn anything about HTML.

The second feature is that the site can keep track of visitors who are "members". Users can register on the site to become a member and they are then given a personalized membership profile.

So what? Well, it allows the MOZI site to do advanced things that aren't obvious to normal site visitors. For example, the site can be configured so that if a member logs in and the system sees they are flagged as a wholesale client all the prices on the site change to wholesale prices automatically! All other users see normal retail prices but the wholesale client sees special pricing reserved just for them. So wholesalers don't have to get MOZI on the phone to check wholesale pricing or place a wholesale order, because their order can go in directly on the public website but still give them the benefit of wholesale pricing: a big convenience for wholesalers and a huge labor saving for MOZI who don't have to spend as much time answering the phone for routine questions.

Being a dynamic site it's also much easier to keep updated than a traditional site. When MOZI staff need to update details of a product on the site they can just log to a Content Management System (CMS) that lets them add, edit and delete products directly from their web browser. They can also create newsletters and publish news items on the site using the same system, and upload images and PDF files to be associated with specific products. They can also edit content such as the home page, company profile, stockist list, and frequently asked questions right in their browser – all without needing to know a single thing about HTML.

Because the Content Management System allows them to make all the changes through their web browser, all MOZI need is a computer connected to the Internet in order to keep their site up to date. There's no software to install and they can update the site from anywhere at any time.

The site management software also includes a sophisticated Customer Relationship Management system (CRM) which can act as the central contact database for the business. It allows contacts to be segmented according to arbitrary categories such as type of customer. Newsletters and product updates can then be automatically sent to relevant customers based on their segmentation, and interactions such as phone calls can be logged for future reference.

For example, some customers could be flagged as a "wholesaler". Then when a special promotion is about to be run a personalized email could be sent just to dealers to let them know that they should order more stock, then later another personalized email could be sent to all retail customers telling them about the promo and where they can go to make a purchase.

This gives MOZI a very powerful tool for managing relationships with both wholesale and retail clients.

Agilent Customer Education Program

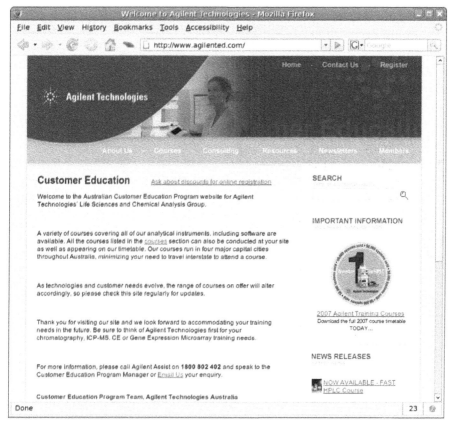

Site: **Agilent Customer Education Program**

URL: www.agilented.com

Agilent has a very active customer education program and runs a wide range of courses covering many different topics. At any time there might be several dozen courses scheduled with many hundreds of participants.

Agilent therefore had a twofold problem: providing a public-facing system for people to learn about courses and sign up for them, and an inward-facing system to allow Agilent staff to keep track of course bookings, payments, and course prerequisites. To meet these requirements the Agilent Customer Education Program website consists of both public and private sections.

The public site allows members of the public to browse a list of pending courses, read course outlines, and see what venues and dates are scheduled. They can also reserve places in upcoming courses directly on the website, and once registered for a course they receive automatic email reminders just prior to commencement so they don't forget to attend. They can also put themselves on waiting lists for courses that have already been filled in case a withdrawal occurs or a repeat of the course is scheduled.

However, the public side of the site is just the tip of the iceberg. The private side forms a complex event management and contact tracking system for Agilent staff, allowing them to keep track of a large number of events and attendees from any computer with a web browser. By logging into a secure private area they can use their browser to schedule a new course and have it appear immediately on the public site, track registrations on a course by course basis, look up contact details for any course attendee, put courses on hold or reschedule them, generate PDF brochures for each course, set course pricing, and more.

Better still, the private section of the site incorporates a CRM (Customer Relationship Management) system which allows Agilent staff to manage their contact database online. As a result they don't need to run address book software on their local computers, they can access the contact database from the office or at home using any computer with a web browser. The CRM allows them to define contact categories and then classify contacts to allow specific subsets to be displayed. For example, categories could be defined for geographic areas and different types of equipment, and all customers who buy a piece of equipment are classified according to the equipment type and their location. Then later when a course about a particular type of equipment is going to be scheduled it's a simple matter for Agilent staff to generate a list of all clients in that geographic area who have bought that equipment in the past, and then contact them to promote the course.

This allows Agilent to be much more specific about how they interact with their clients, since each client can be provided information which is particularly relevant to them.

The Agilented site is a good example of the way modern websites are rapidly moving away from being simple brochures and are becoming complex pieces of software which provide real business functionality. The difference is that unlike traditional software it's accessed through a web browser rather than running on a local computer like normal software.

Public Relations Institute of Australia

Site: **Public Relations Institute of Australia**

URL: www.pria.com.au

The Public Relations Institute of Australia is an industry association that provides a variety of services to members, including professional development courses; books; training materials; networking events; and industry news and updates.

The site is primarily a resource for association members and therefore has "members only" sections. While anyone can browse the public information on the site, paid-up association members can log in with a username and password to access resources hidden from everyone else. The site also includes an extensive customer relationship management (CRM) system that allows personalized emails to be sent in bulk to members with information about upcoming events or other industry news: a very effective and low-cost way of keeping a large number of association members up to date on the latest developments.

This same concept could be applied to just about any club or association. By using a website with public and private sections an organization can provide members with distinct benefits at minimal cost. Exactly what is provided could vary depending on the nature of the organization: a basketball club could put scores and schedules online, a sailing club could provide a weather feed and a "find a crewmember" service, an industry organization could publish editorials discussing trends and marketing techniques.

Where the PRIA site goes one step further though is by incorporating a comprehensive membership management system. By logging into a password-protected administration area PRIA staff can access a list showing every association member along with relevant information such as their joining / expiry dates and membership level. The system pro-actively tracks which members are about to expire and automatically sends them a  renewal notice with an option to pay online with a credit card, then updates their membership status and sets a new expiry date automatically when payment has been made. This saves PRIA staff a huge amount of administrative effort by allowing the membership database to almost take care of itself. Managing a membership database is probably one of the biggest ongoing burdens on a typical industry association so automating the process frees up staff to work productively on other tasks.

The PRIA site also demonstrates a very important principle: sites which build up a community of users and allow interaction between them can be far more successful than sites which treat each user as an isolated individual. Providing users with a sense of community and shared purpose can make your site extremely popular.

Shaver Shop

Site:	**Shaver Shop public website and franchise extranet**
URL:	www.shavershop.com.au

Shaver Shop is a franchise-based business that specializes in retail sales of personal grooming products and has dozens of stores throughout Australia. Shaver Shop wanted a website that would service two very distinct audiences with totally different requirements: consumers and franchisees.

But that introduced a big problem because like most wholesalers and franchise operators they face a difficult balancing act. Bypassing existing distribution layers ("dis-intermediation" in industry jargon) by providing products and services directly to consumers is a common way to squeeze down retail prices, but it also makes enemies of those who sell your product for you because they feel they are in competition with their own supplier. The last thing a franchiser wants to do is anger franchisees by allowing consumers to bypass them.

However, that has to be balanced against the increasing demand from consumers for access to product information online. Put on too much information or sell directly online and franchisees get mad because they feel cut out of the loop. Put on too little information and consumers become frustrated and go to a competitor. Not a good situation for a franchiser!

Shaver Shop solved the problem in a very neat way: they created a site which provides detailed product information including prices, and even allows users to order directly from the website – but rather than cut franchisees out of the loop, all online orders are automatically assigned to a franchisee near the customer's delivery address based on agreed franchise regions. When a customer goes to the Shaver Shop site and places an order they are asked to provide billing and delivery information, including their postcode. Order management software running behind the scenes accepts the order, then compares the customer's postcode to a list of franchise regions to find the closest retail store. The order is then tagged as assigned to that store, the product is shipped to the customer, the store receives an order rebate and everyone is happy. The customer is happy because they received their order, Shaver Shop is happy because a sale was made, and the franchisee is happy because they received payment for a sale with very little effort.

That's a very clever solution to a common problem, and it could be applied to just about any business which has distribution layers between the supplier and the customer. For example, a bicycle wholesaler could make online sales directly to customers and assign a percentage of each sale to the closest retail store. The customer could also be alerted to the fact that the sale was assigned to a store, encouraging them to become a customer of the store directly when the time comes for add-on sales such as accessories.

The other important aspect of the Shaver Shop site is the franchise extranet. Franchisees are given a username and password to access the extranet, and once logged in they can use a variety of tools designed to help them grow their business. For example, they can select products from the Shaver Shop range and specify a price discount for each one, and the extranet immediately generates PDF files they can use to print shelf tags using a variety of templates. This ensures that all stores have  a consistent appearance to their in-store tags while allowing them to generate new tags with custom prices as required.

The extranet also contains a photo gallery of store decorations and displays, and allows franchisees to upload photos of their own stores. This provides a valuable collaboration opportunity for franchisees to work together to improve their store presentation. It also includes a list of orders which have been assigned to their store and allows them to check rebate reconciliations, order status, and shipping details.

One of the other interesting things Shaver Shop do with their website is create short-term "landing pages" related to special promotions and competitions. More about these later!

2. In-House Or Outsource?
Passing the buck

So you want a website for your company, but should you have your own people develop it in-house or should you outsource the job to a professional web developer?

It depends on many factors of course, but the best approach is usually a combination of both with internal staff providing most of the content for your site and an external developer handling creation of the graphics, HTML, scripts, databases and other technical aspects.

A lot of people have the idea that they would like to do all the development in-house, and for some projects that may be the best way to go. It's a decision you must make based on your specific circumstances, but it really comes down to one question: do you want to become a pro web developer yourself?

Value your time

Because it's deceptively simple to create basic web pages using tools like FrontPage and Dreamweaver it can be very tempting to think that you can save money by creating a whole company site yourself. To be honest, putting together web pages using tools like these is not rocket science. Anyone who can use a word processor should be able to figure out the basics of driving Dreamweaver in a fairly short time, and there are no end of "create your own homepage" books.

However, as you'll discover by reading this book there is a world of difference between putting together a basic personal site and creating a fully-functional corporate website. Considering the huge amount of time required to master the intricacies of web development it would almost always be cheaper to hire a developer to do the job for you. If you truly consider your own time to be worth something, thinking about how much there is to learn on the subject is a daunting thought.

Of course, it may sound like I'm biased (I am a web developer, after all!) but think about this: if you wanted to run a series of TV ads, would you handle all the writing, the camera work, the acting, the voice-over, the set creation, the editing, and the airtime purchase personally? Probably not. There are many people who do exactly that (I can think of a certain local lighting company and several mobile phone dealers, for example!) but the results very rarely project a professional image. And by the time you've bought and learned how to use all the equipment, it probably would have been cheaper to hire professionals anyway.

But when it comes to creating websites people often take the DIY approach.

One reason is they think they can build a site after-hours and don't allow for the large amount of time that will be required, and don't put a dollar value on their own time so they think they can create a site "for free".

Another reason is that the average person doesn't really understand what makes a site good or bad, and they don't have the knowledge or experience to make a distinction. When they whip something up in FrontPage in half an hour, they think it's as good as something created by a pro development company that allocated several person-months to the job and implemented a complete CRM and CMS. It's like that DIY television ad creator who thinks their ad looks as professional as one created by an experienced production house. They may be starry-eyed about their own creation, but to everyone else it just looks cheap and tacky.

How much do sites cost?

So how much does a professionally developed website cost anyway?

That's obviously a very hard question to answer (how long is a piece of string?), but since 1996 BtoB have tried to determine indicative pricing by presenting hypothetical scenarios to a number of developers and obtaining quotes on them. BtoB regularly reports the results in the Web Price Index, accessible online at www.businessmarketing.com/

Take those figures with a grain (or cup!) of salt, though. In my experience the prices given in the Web Price Index are on the high side. The May 2000 study gave the median cost of developing a typical site at US$113,500 – for what they class as a typical website!

Of course a lot has happened since May 2000 and I'm sure a similar survey now would indicate significantly lower figures for similar projects.

Budgeting for your website should be an iterative process that takes place in consultation with your developer, aimed at getting the most appropriate bang for the minimum buck based on your specific objectives.

I'll get to that process in a later chapter.

3. Staffing
Who's who in the zoo

There are many different roles in the development of a corporate website. Sometimes several roles can be handled by one person. Some are best handled in-house, and for others you may require an external contractor. For most projects the best option will be a combination of internal staffing for most content development while retaining the services of an external developer for site planning, design, production and promotion.

The following guide is not a hard and fast rule, and may vary depending on your internal resources and the size of the developer. Labels may vary from place to place, but it does give a good overview of the many roles involved. Some of these roles may be duplicated: for example, there may be many Production Specialists covering various disciplines. Web development teams can vary from one to hundreds of people, but for a typical small to medium project my company generally has around four to eight people involved at different stages.

Your internal staff

Website Manager

The Website Manager should not be expected to write a single line of code or create even the smallest graphic. The Website Manager's role is to coordinate development from the client side, to oversee the direction and progress of the site, to ensure content deadlines are met by internal sources, to review design and content drafts, and to liaise with your developer.

It's very important that your Website Manager is clearly understood to be the primary liaison person with your developer to prevent conflicting requirements being conveyed. This is often a problem internally, as there may be a tendency for additional people to jump into the project part way through and want their departmental or personal interests made a high priority. Make sure that as the project progresses the same person remains the Website Manager and all communication is filtered through them. This doesn't mean that no-one else is allowed to talk to the developer's staff, just that the Website Manager needs to stay hands-on throughout the project. This is a very important rule: breaking it is one of the major reasons that website development projects end up with feature-bloat, behind schedule and over budget.

Contributors

Contributors are responsible for providing internally supplied content, which may be product information, images, technical articles, support resources, database files, and anything else your developer will need from you to do their job. Keeping contributors on track will probably be your biggest headache, because delays in providing material can cause ripple-down problems for the entire project as a result of what developers call "dependencies". Contributors can actually be broken down into several sub-categories based on areas of responsibility, but we'll get to that in Chapter 16: *Content.*

The developer's staff

Project Manager

This role may alternatively be known as the Producer or Production Manager in studio-type development agencies. This is the equivalent position to your Website Manager, but within the developer's organization. During development almost all contact between your organization and your developer will be your Website Manager talking to the developer's Project Manager.

Account Executive

The Account Executive is your primary liaison before and after the site is actually produced. The Account Executive's role is to look at the overall business model of your company and act as your advocate within the developer's organization, but they are not involved with the technical aspects of the site's production. In smaller development companies or for smaller projects the Project Manager and the Account Executive may be the same person.

Information Architect

An Information Architect (sometimes called an Information Designer) is responsible for determining the structure into which the site contents will be placed. An Information Architect will typically be interested in user objectives and how to structure the site so users can achieve those objectives in the simplest way possible. Note that an Information Architect often couldn't care less about the graphical look of the site: they think more in terms of "blocks" or "chunks" of information, and the best way to sequence those blocks. The work of the Information Architect determines the sections that will be created in the final site and the navigation that will allow users to move around between those sections.

Marketing Consultant

The Marketing Consultant will provide input on the purpose and target audience of the project, and may advise on the site launch and post-launch promotional activities. They will also oversee any market research which needs to be undertaken, including focus group sessions and compilation of statistics.

Design Manager

The Design Manager may also be called the Creative Director or similar. They manage the overall "look and feel" of the site, and coordinate the work of the Designers. The Design Manager acts as a filter, deciding which designs to show you and which to reject or send back to the Designers for reworking, and co-ordinates the various designers working on each project.

Designers

The Designers initially develop the rough image concepts or "comps" (composites) for approval by the Design Manager and then the Project Manager. Once a design direction has been decided on, the Designers create all the different graphics and images required for the final site, plus any banners or associated design work which may be required for promotion. Design for the web has a whole new set of rules compared to print, so don't expect a print designer to produce for the web without significant additional training.

Production Specialists

There are so many areas of specialization related to Internet development that no one person can know it all. Many web developers employ or sub-contract specialists in fields such as usability research, vector animation, audio recording and streaming, video editing and production, 3D modeling, CGI programming, virtual reality systems, databases and many others.

Database Developer

A few years ago a Database Developer had little place on a web development team. Today they are almost indispensable, because even the smallest sites can use dynamic data to make updates and management simpler. A Database Developer is really a production specialist, but they are now so fundamental in determining the overall functionality of most modern websites that they rank with the Design Manager. For complex projects there will probably be a Database Manager with several Database Developers working under them. At my company almost all projects involve input from three or more Database

Developers, since we focus strongly on creating sites with dynamic content.

Copy Writers

Text for your website needs to be written quite differently to text for other media. Copy writing for the web is now a specialist field in it's own right, as will be explained in Chapter 17: *Writing For The Web*.

Technical Writers

Documentation is one area that is often overlooked by web developers. Internal documentation can be as simple as defining the file structure on the server so members of the production team can find things easily, but external documentation is often required as well. For example, you may require documentation for your site administrators to explain how to handle product updates, price changes etc on the website.

System Administrator

Responsibilities of the System Administrator (sysadmin) include running the public and staging web servers and the production file server, making sure all the developer's computers run smoothly, keeping the network going, installing new software and streamlining manual processes where possible. System Administrators are absolutely fundamental to the development of a website, but if everything goes smoothly they will work pro-actively in the background and you'll probably never even realize they exist. An invisible sysadmin is a good sysadmin.

Office Administrator

While all the development staff are hard at work on your site someone needs to make sure the bills are paid and accounts are kept up to date. Web developers with more than a couple of staff quickly find they need at least one office administrator to keep everything on track and make sure the phones aren't disconnected.

4. Types Of Developers
They come in many flavors...

Because the web is still a relatively young medium it doesn't have a long history of generations of developers refining their processes and educating customers over the years. The web itself was only invented in 1989, with the first early adopters taking up residence over the next couple of years and commercialization not really beginning until about 1994. That's only yesterday in historical terms! In almost any industry you can find companies that have been around for at least dozens and sometimes hundreds of years, but not in the web development industry.

What does this mean for you? Well, a few things.

First, it means that answering the question "What is a web developer?" is actually a lot harder than it sounds. As you'll see, there are a huge variety of individuals and organizations calling themselves web developers. Their abilities vary as dramatically as their backgrounds.

Second, it means that you can't rely so much on established brands or long history to decide whether the developer doing a pitch to you today will still be in business tomorrow. You will need to assess potential developers with a critical eye and at least a little understanding of what it is you expect them to do for you.

Third, and to complicate the previous point, you as the client may not have built up years of experience in dealing with web developers to know what to expect. When you visit your accountant, or your doctor, or even a graphic designer to put together a brochure, you probably have a good idea what the basic procedure is going to be. But how accurate are your expectations of your web developer?

What I'll do in this chapter is briefly outline the kinds of companies you are likely to come across who call themselves web developers.

Advertising agency

In the early days of the commercialization of the Internet, a number of advertising agencies jumped all over what they saw (correctly) as an enormous new market and set up "new media" departments. These agencies brought all the razzle-dazzle of their industry to the process of web development, along with expectations of big fees and large project teams.

A lot of the early high profile commercial sites were put together by advertising agencies whose first move was to target their existing large clients with glitzy pitches that put all their competition to shame. Because of their history with their clients they effectively owned the accounts, and the smaller, more specialist developers didn't get a look in. In the end that wasn't necessarily a bad thing, because a lot of the technical work was subcontracted out to specialist developers anyway and the overall level of professionalism of all developers was given a standard to be judged against. Possibly the only people who lost out were the clients who ended up spending a lot more in the short term than they strictly needed to. Any site created in the mid 90's with a 7-figure price tag was almost certainly contracted to an advertising agency.

Advertising agencies are traditionally very good at managing client relationships, and tend to look at that relationship not as a one-off sale but as a partnership for life. However, all the fancy lunches they invite you to have to come out of someone's pocket eventually – probably yours!

Ma 'n' Pa web shop

There are a large number of sole traders, small partnerships, freelance developers and husband and wife teams providing web development services either full time or as a side-line to another small business, such as a graphic design business or computer shop.

These sorts of developers can be very good value for smaller jobs, provided you begin the project with a good understanding of what you expect to achieve and know the limitations of the developer. As you saw in Chapter 3: *Staffing* there are a huge range of roles and responsibilities in a web project. Finding one individual who can do all those things well is a big task. The best situation is someone who can handle the project management on your behalf and perhaps the design work, page layout and HTML, and can call on associates or partner companies for other specific tasks such as database development and coding. This approach can work quite well provided the principal developer has a realistic understanding of their own abilities and limitations, and can accurately assess the time and costs involved in the aspects of the project they may need to outsource.

Solo freelance developers come from a variety of backgrounds but they are most typically graphic designers who moved sideways into web design and therefore have good creativity but may have only average technical expertise. Some come from a programming or system administration background and have strong technical skills, but minimal design training or ability.

And of course there is the rare find, a truly multi-talented individual who can do everything well from start to finish. But believe me, they are *really* hard to find, and if you do find one to put your site together you may be out of luck six months down the track when you want to do updates. Freelance developers tend to go through very deep famine-feast cycles and have extremely variable availability, and if they are really skilled they often end up working full-time at a bigger development company leaving you with no-one to provide ongoing maintenance and support. One of the most common stories that web developers hear from new clients goes something like "We had this hotshot freelance developer build our site for us, and he did a great job but now he's gone to work for some big company and no-one knows how to make changes to our site."

Graphic design house

Like advertising agencies, graphic design houses tend to be very account-oriented and try to manage their client relationships as an on-going partnership. Because they have existing revenue and contacts as a result of non-Internet design projects they can be in a good position to move sideways into providing web development services. This can work out well for you because they can often provide a broader design service than a specialist web developer, tying together your online and off-line media in a cohesive way.

However, they tend to be fairly weak in technical ability and often partner with specialist subcontractors for specific sections of many projects. There's nothing wrong with that though as long as the project manager keeps a close eye on all the players and the parties involved work well together and remain well coordinated.

Internet consultant

One type of developer that has become more common in recent years is the Internet consultant who may come to you with a great pitch, manage your project from start to finish, and then deliver the product at the end of the day but not do a single minute of development work themselves. Many even pass themselves off as running a large development agency, but just call in subcontractors to do everything – and the client is none the wiser.

This can work extremely well, or it can be a disaster.

Provided the consultant actually has (successful!) experience with managing web projects and a good relationship with all the subcontractors required, they may be able to come in and work as a hired gun to get the job done in a very efficient way. Because they don't have the overhead of employing specialist staff when not required they can cut costs and shop around for deals with specialist subcontractors on your behalf while providing you with a single person to deal with for project management issues.

But many solo Internet consultants promise the world but can't deliver the goods. The danger is a consultant who is all theory and no experience, and dramatically underestimates the requirements of your project. I had an experience recently where an Internet consultant provided a proposal and quote to a client, then after they got the job they came to my company for a quote on the cost of actually implementing it (yes, I know that was doing things backwards!). The specification document was quite extensive, and our initial estimate put the basic cost at somewhere in the region of $50,000. We later learned the consultant had budgeted only $4,500 for the entire implementation, and was desperately trying to find a subcontractor to do the job at that price so he wouldn't blow the project. No wonder he got the job if he quoted less than 10% of what the price should have been!

Amazingly that particular story had a happy ending, but those sorts of mistakes usually cause spectacular meltdowns. You don't want to be in a similar situation, trust me. If you're dealing with a supplier who can't actually handle your project in-house you should be extremely careful.

The neighbor's son's classmate

No, I'm not kidding. There's a whole category that needs to be devoted to high school students who are asked to create websites "because they learned HTML at school, and they'll be cheap." Throw 'em a couple of hundred bucks (which will seem like a fortune to them), wait a while, get a website.

It goes without saying that the end result probably won't be too crash hot. I'm not saying that the neighbor's son's classmate can't graduate to being a high-flying developer at a prestigious company in a couple of years, or even that they don't know their stuff right now, just that they probably don't have the experience, the breadth of skills or the resources to pull off anything more than a fairly basic job. And if you've got an urgent problem during business hours, you may be out of luck.

Integrated developer

Almost all the previous examples were of individuals or businesses who have moved sideways into web development from some other field and may still see web development as just a nice little sideline. An integrated developer, on the other hand, is a web development company whose primary reason for existence is Internet projects. They typically employ from 5 to maybe a hundred staff, and have in-house expertise covering almost every aspect of site development. Their staff usually cover every role listed in Chapter 3: *Staffing*.

Integrated developers generally form project teams for each project, with the specific staffing composition varying over the life of the project. As various projects progress at different rates and through different stages their staff may move from one project to another as required. This allows them to maintain specialists in-house who simply would not be economically viable for other types of organizations.

They may also be able to provide related services such as website hosting internally. At the very least they'll have all the necessary business relationships in place and be able to manage such things on your behalf.

Integrated developers are the workhorses of the industry. When an advertising agency needs to provide a shopping cart system to a client, or a graphic design house needs to provide credit card transactions, or an Internet consultant needs anything at all, that's who they'll turn to.

The mega-developer

A notable event in the web industry has been the formation of mega-developers with thousands of staff and annual billings measured in the tens or hundreds of millions of US$. They are mainly the result of mergers between many smaller integrated developers, advertising agencies and software houses trying to cut costs and land bigger clients through consolidation and economies of scale, such as Scient and marchFIRST. Some are formed as consulting arms of existing mega-corporations, such as IBM Global Services. Great if you have a web project with a 7 figure budget and need a developer scaled to suit!

Unfortunately mega-developers seem to be no more stable than any other type of developer, with spectacular failures like marchFIRST showing that sometimes being big (or huge, in this case) is not necessarily enough.

The great developer die-back

After several years of a fluid, unstable and varied industry floating on the hopes of the dot-coms, web developers have come back to Earth with a crash. 2001-2002 saw dramatic changes, and specialized developers without a diversified income were hit hard. Big integrated developers (those with maybe 100+ staff) had everything against them: lots of expensive specialist staff with wages inflated by the unrealistic expectations of dot-com stocks, a client base consisting of doomed Internet ventures, and absolutely no other revenue streams.

The most canny (and agile) developers realized that the days of brochureware websites were numbered and re-invented themselves more along the lines of software development houses if they weren't merged up into the coalescing mega-developers. In fact, the strongest web developers in the US are now the medium (10 to 90 staff) integrated developers who think of the web not just as a place for pretty pictures but as a delivery medium for sophisticated software such as CRMs, intranets, extranets and dynamic websites. The equivalent in my hometown of Melbourne, Australia is integrated developers in the 5 to 30 staff range.

5. Obtaining Quotes
Everyone, take your partner's hand...

Most people use totally the wrong approach when searching for a company to develop their website. Selecting a web developer is not just a matter of finding a group who can meet your technical requirements or that has the lowest quote. They need to be a match for you on a business and even personal level as well. A shopping-list of software they know how to drive and programming languages their staff work with is not enough. How well they work with your organization is critical.

A typical (but wrong!) approach is to do a bit of homework to decide what features are required for the site, put it down on paper (perhaps in the form of an RFP, or Request For Proposal) and have a number of developers quote on it. An assessment is then made on the basis of the 3 Ps: price, presentation and precedents. The problem with this approach is the first level of filtering is done on the basis of prices on a pre-specified solution, and you ignore the potential for alternative solutions to your problem from people who should know your options better than you do yourself.

A better approach is to look first and foremost for a developer with whom you can work comfortably. Go and visit them, don't just have them come to you. Get a feel for their culture, their working environment, their staff, their attitude. Make sure they have the technical ability to do the job, and look at their folio. Many smaller developers have limited design resources or skill, and may have a very characterized "look" to all their sites. Developers who come from a purely graphic-design background may not have the database and system administration skills necessary to handle the technical aspects of your project. Find someone that can fit in with how you want the site to look and your technical and feature requirements, and can work within your budgetary guidelines. The right developer will work to provide the best solution within your specific restrictions, financial and otherwise.

Where do you find them?

I still think that one of the best ways to find a good developer is by word of mouth. If you know people who have had sites created, ask them who did the development and how well the process went. Also ask about ongoing support – did the developer create the site and then vanish, or did they build an ongoing relationship with the site owner and continue to work with them to make the site a success?

If you find sites that have similar features and scope to what you have in mind, why not just ask who created them? You can often find out who created a specific site by dropping a quick email to the site owner, possibly even asking them about their experiences (both good and bad) with the developer.

While word of mouth is often the best, other good old-fashioned approaches include checking in your local Yellow Pages (online of course, does anyone use the dead-tree edition nowadays?) or with your local Chamber of Commerce. Just searching online probably won't help overly much because the search engines will give you a huge number of results (Google gave me 29 million results on a search for "web developer" last time I checked!) but if you narrow the results down by including your city or region you may find some possibilities.

How do you assess them?

So you have 37 different web developers jostling for the job of developing or updating your website, and they all seem to have strengths and weaknesses. How do you tell them apart? How do you decide which to go with?

The very first thing you need to do is narrow the contenders down to just the ones who are capable of actually doing the job you have in mind. As you saw in the last chapter, developers come in all shapes and sizes. Some went into business last week, some have an enviable track record, and some will by gone by tomorrow. Cross off your list any that aren't available in your time frame due to other project commitments or who cannot demonstrate the ability to deliver on jobs like yours. And I **mean** demonstrate, not just say they think they can handle it! If yours is the biggest project they've ever done you should be extremely careful.

Next, having pre-qualified the initial contenders down to a list of just the developers who would be capable of actually doing the job, you need to consider the "fit factors": the things that indicate how well each developer fits your requirements.

A good way to manage this part of the selection process is to use a developer selection matrix, whereby you specify a number of assessment criteria and then assign developers a score for each item. David Siegel included a simple developer selection matrix in *Secrets Of Successful Websites*, where he provides excellent commentary on both good and bad approaches to finding a web developer. I've updated David's matrix to place more emphasis on the technical and organizational skills commonly required for modern sites and extended it with score breakdowns for different areas of expertise. My updated version of the matrix lets you see exactly how various developers stack up against each other with respect to criteria such as project management ability, design strength, and technical strength.

You can see my version of the matrix at the end of this book in Appendix C: *Developer Selection Matrix*, and I've also created a spreadsheet version which you can download from the book site at www.stay-sane.com/developermatrix. The spreadsheet makes it particularly easy – just punch in the scores for each of the criteria and the spreadsheet will show you a total score at the end plus breakdowns by section.

Using the developer selection matrix is very simple and I highly recommend that you try it out even if your project is small or you are only assessing one developer. Seeing the scores come out at the end can be a very educational experience, and may indicate unexpected areas of strength and weakness in the developers trying to win your business.

However, even if you decide not to use such a formal process you should still very carefully assess the contenders with several factors in mind.

The first major issue to consider is their project management expertise. In my opinion this is one of the most important things for a developer to get right. If they can't manage their projects well, which includes issues such as providing good scope documents and planning their internal resource availability, it doesn't matter how good they are technically or what nice people they are. Great technicians working without a plan will probably make a mess of whatever they put their hand to, but average technicians working under a great project manager can achieve amazing things. Check whether the developer has a structured methodology and well understood processes, and whether they understand the need to manage projects carefully and communicate well.

As I mentioned previously I think cultural fit is another very important factor. Do they understand your industry, or at least show an interest in it and a willingness to learn? Do they understand you and communicate well with you? Imagine you were hiring the staff of this firm as employees – would you want to work in the same office as them? Don't take this too far though. You're not trying to make friends for life: you're paying a supplier to do a specific job. But in my experience things always work better when the different parties get along well.

Next consider their ability and skill set. By this I don't mean just knowledge of

HTML, but also things like whether they use a formal development process, the ability of their designers to work to your requirements, the depth of their database expertise if it is necessary for your site (in my opinion it's necessary for every modern site), their ability to provide marketing and post-launch support, and all the other services you would expect as part of the development process. This is where a selection matrix can really help you make sense of the differences between otherwise similar developers.

Finally consider the cost of working with each company. It's a fact of life that there are Fords and Ferraris, and even if you want a Ferrari website you may only have the budget for a Ford developer. Be realistic and consider which developer will give you the most bang for the bucks you have available. Also keep in mind issues of ongoing costs such as site updates and hosting. A developer who can create a site with a Content Management System (more about these later!) may charge more up front, but with the long-term benefit that you can update the site yourself at any time without additional expense. As with most things in life, something cheap now may be more expensive in the long run.

"Free" quotes and economic reality

About once or twice each week I get an email out of the blue from someone with an outline for a project they want quoted. The funny thing is there are sometimes anything from 10 to 50 other developers' addresses listed in the "To" field of the email. What are these people thinking? Do they expect all 50 developers to send them a detailed quote and project plan? They obviously haven't gone through the process I just mentioned of narrowing down the list to only pre-qualified potential developers before asking for quotes.

Who do they think pays for all the "free" quotes they obtain? They do in the end, and anyone else who retains a web developer. Providing quotes and responding to RFPs is an overhead that all developers must carry, and like any other industry it's necessary to either pass overheads on to clients or go out of business. That's just harsh reality.

Think of it this way. Imagine you are the marketing manager of a mid size enterprise, and you want to obtain quotes on having a site created or updated. Being very careful to retain the best possible developer for the project you outline a project specification and present it to 10 different developers. You ask each of them to prepare a detailed proposal including their intended approach to the project and a cost breakdown.

Each of those developers then has an account manager spend 10 hours researching your business, formulating a preliminary project plan, evaluating the costs and preparing a proposal. Each of those developers therefore incurs an on-cost of 10 hours plus materials. Average labor cost in a business like web development (which must offset high hardware and software costs and rapid asset depreciation) is about 1.7 times the wage, so if the account manager is on an extremely conservative $25/hour the developers have each incurred a cost of $425 just to respond to your request for a quote. Add in materials (stationery, postage, travel, promotional CD, brochures, etc) and the figure will easily top $500. It may sound like an unrealistically big number, but even $500 is probably a low estimate: one pitch my company did recently cost us over $4000 including two interstate trips and several weeks of background research.

Then, consider that you asked 10 developers to quote. If each proposal conservatively costs $500 to prepare and each developer can only win an average of one contract in 10 that they quote on, they'll be spending $5000 doing pitches for each contract they win. And if these costs aren't covered they'll go bankrupt, so effectively $5000 has to be added to the cost of every job they win.

Please don't imagine for a second that I'm saying you should only ever obtain one quote, or that you should retain a developer without demanding they do their homework first. As the customer you are entitled to clear, accurate and detailed quotes from your suppliers and you are certainly entitled to make absolutely sure you are partnering with the right group. Go ahead and make prospective suppliers jump through flaming hoops over crocodile pits in order to win your job, but first make sure you pre-qualify your list of potential developers.

Take the developer selection process seriously – don't just spam 50 developers with a request for a quote and expect 50 well crafted responses.

Focus on needs, not technology

Something I often see in RFPs and in meetings with potential clients is a focus on technology rather than business requirements. It seems there is an unwritten rule that all RFPs must include the sentence "consideration must be given to utilizing the latest technologies to showcase our cutting-edge products while still allowing the greatest possible number of users to access the site".

Of course we all want sites that load in the blink of an eye, feature full motion video and work with every browser version ever released, but specifying that in the RFP isn't going to make it happen.

The RFP should specify what the project is intended to achieve at a business level, who will be using your site, and for what purpose: do you want to make the site easily accessible to all possible users, perhaps at the expense of a bit of eye candy? Or are you willing to raise the barrier to entry to the site and possibly lose some visitors so you can use advanced technology like Flash to add a bit of sizzle? Given this sort of information the designer can choose the most appropriate technology for your purpose rather than bending inappropriate tech to a poorly defined purpose. If your developer is worth their salt they will have a far better understanding of the options than you, so you should concentrate on specifying what you want to achieve from a business perspective and then let the selection of technology logically follow on from that. Any other approach is putting the cart before the horse.

6. Contracts And Documentation
Two-way protection

Unfortunately it's a fact of business that contracts are often required in order to legally protect both parties to an agreement. However, contracts don't need to be a major stumbling block - the important thing is to make sure there is a written agreement that specifies who is responsible for what. If a web developer wants you to sign a contract with them it's a sign they take the project seriously and don't want any misunderstandings down the track. Conversely, if the developer shies away from the idea of a contract or a detailed project specification it may be a sign they are unsure of their ability to do the job.

The kind of contracts used will vary from developer to developer and country to country, as different countries have different laws that must be taken into account. However, contract law is similar in most Western countries so the contracts in this section will probably be relevant wherever you are.

The legal documentation of an Internet project protects both parties for different reasons. Your developer wants to be sure they are going to be paid for work performed, and you want to know the job will be completed as agreed and that you will not be overcharged or caught out with copyright issues.

Different contracts are used at different stages of the process. The following are examples of the contracts my company often uses.

Non-disclosure agreement

If my company is doing a pitch to a prospective client and we have a design, a technology, a business concept or a marketing idea that we believe is unique or gives us a competitive edge, we may require the prospective client to sign a non-disclosure agreement (NDA). This agreement protects us from being ripped off by companies who troll for detailed proposals, distill all the good ideas from them and then develop the site in-house or give the ideas to another developer. In this form the NDA is structured to protect the developer, with the developer as the "discloser" and the client as the "recipient" of the information.

During the process of creating your site your developer may have reason to come into contact with material you feel is sensitive or should not be distributed other than as required to complete the project. This could include items like trade pricing, information on product suppliers or costs, and anything else you would not want publicly distributed. In this case an NDA may be used which protects you as the client, and will be essentially the same as the NDA mentioned above but with your developer as the "recipient" and you as the "discloser".

One common variation on the theme is a mutual non-disclosure agreement, which basically binds both parties to protect each others secrets and is equivalent to each party having an NDA to bind the other.

Project scope / synopsis

While not a legal contract in a strict sense, the project scope / synopsis document defines what will be provided by the developer and when. It may also cover some responsibilities of the client, for example specifying dates for delivery of certain source material. This document is effectively the blueprint for the sequence of events that will come together as the new website, and so is very important.

My company's project scope / synopsis documents are generally broken down into several major sections, including:

The "Project Objectives" section defines why the project is being undertaken, what outcomes are expected, and what the ROI (Return On Investment) should be.

The "Functionality" section defines what the site will specifically do in order to achieve those objectives. It is a fairly detailed description of what users will be able to do on the site.

The "Deliverables" section defines what we will supply to the client as the finished product in order to achieve that functionality. It includes a list of the major sections of the site, what functions each will have, etc. If the project is to be undertaken in a number of stages it will also include the sequence of development, indicating which sections will be delivered in each stage.

The "Client Responsibilities" section lists what materials the client must supply to the developer, such as product information, catalog images, etc.

Quotation

The Quotation is a fairly standard document, including details of what will be charged for each stage of the project, any deposit or stage payments which may be required, and the projected dates for completion of each stage. It may also include charges for additional services such as hosting fees, domain name registration, license fees for special software or images required for your project, and other ancillary costs.

For the convenience of our clients we usually combine the Project Scope / Synopsis and the Quotation into a single document which we call the Proposal. The Proposal is therefore a concise overview of the project from technical, chronological and financial perspectives.

Purchase order

Your developer will need something in writing to specify that you accept the details of their proposal, authorizing them to begin work and incurring expenses on your behalf. A simple purchase order is generally sufficient, and should be signed and faxed or snail mailed to your developer. For work to begin my company also generally requires a deposit to be paid at the same time as the purchase order is presented – standard practice in the industry.

Change orders

Any changes to the specifications outlined in the project scope / synopsis document should be formally recorded using change orders. A change order is a brief document that acts as an addendum to the original project scope / synopsis, and will probably also result in adjustments to the quotation.

For example, you may decide that you wish to add an extra section to the site to accommodate a feature not allowed for at the time the project scope / synopsis was drafted. Depending on how far the project has progressed this may have several effects. In a worst case scenario the navigation and interface design may have already been finalized and the graphics implemented, in which case the original design may have to be revised to accommodate new navigational items. Back-end databases may also have to be redesigned.

There will almost always be additional costs incurred as a result of a change order. Even if the change involves removal of a section that was included in the original project scope / synopsis, this may mean revising an already finalized interface design to remove some navigational elements.

Management of change orders is one of the biggest headaches for web developers because of the issue of dependencies. Web development is a largely linear process, with each stage dependent on the prior stages. If the developer has reached a late point in the development process and a change order comes in which has a major effect on a very early stage, they may have to go almost back to the start of the project and rework each intermediate stage.

Change orders are usually cumulative: they cannot be deleted or canceled, but a subsequent change order may cancel the effects of a previous one. That makes it easier to look back later and follow the virtual paper trail that the project followed.

Other contracts

There will be times when other legal documents are required, depending on the type and scope of your project.

A **development contract** may be used in place of, or supplemental to, the project scope and purchase order. It will generally define all the deliverables, payment schedule, time frame etc of both parties, condensed into a single legal document that is signed by yourself and your developer. Development contracts are usually used on large projects.

Change orders are used when the scope changes after the project has begun. Changes such as adding a new feature or postponing a section of a site for later development require notice in writing from you to your developer. That way your developer has documentation that the project scope has changed and there are no misunderstandings on what is required for the project or stage to be classified as complete.

A **copyright permission contract** may be used when granting the right to use certain material, such as when using images or sounds which are under copyright.

A **service or maintenance contract** may define ongoing work to be performed, for example to provide regular site maintenance and updates. This contract may also be required to cover maintenance of the web server itself if you are on a dedicated server or relying on an external consultant to manage your own in-house server. If you are intending to enter into a maintenance contract make sure you mention this up front – maintenance contracts are often negotiated with the rest of the job, even though they may not come into effect until the main part of the project has been delivered.

A **letter of intent** (often called a **memorandum of engagement**) is a formal statement that a company intends to enter into a contract with a developer. It's often used as a first step when the developer has been selected but the precise terms of the contract are yet to be finalized.

7. Developer Extranet
Keeping all the little things under control

The process of creating a website can involve a lot of to-and-fro between you and your developer, and it's extremely important to keep the lines of communication open. You need to be sure there's no confusion over issues relating to supply of content, approval of interface designs, requests for functional changes, and all the myriad little things that happen while getting from A to Z.

To make the process easier for their clients some developers use a project management extranet. Extranets are similar to public websites, but are designed for restricted access only by specific external users such as clients and suppliers. Some people also call them "project sites", since they are often set up temporarily for the purpose of managing a specific project.

By logging into a site development extranet you have access to a number of resources to guide you through the project process. Developer extranets can vary dramatically but this guide will give you a broad view of the kinds of things that are typically provided.

Status / Dashboard

The Status / Dashboard section gives an overview of where the project is up to: what stages have been completed, what tasks remain to be completed, etc. It's like a mile-high view of the project.

Project staff

This section provides email links to essential staff, providing a convenient access point for contacting people involved in the project. It may also list areas of responsibility so you can see who to contact for specific issues.

Documents

Copies of all contracts and other documents related to the project held as reference, often in Acrobat (PDF) format. This may include the Project Scope / Synopsis, the Quotation, and any NDAs which have been signed.

Change orders

The change orders section contains a list of all change orders for the project, and may have a form for creation of a new change order. My company's policy is to only accept change orders submitted online through the extranet because that allows us to track exactly who submitted it and when. Many developers also accept change orders by fax, email, or even verbally, although this can make it very difficult to review them down the track.

Design comps

Comps (short for composites) are drafts of the interface for your site. The design comps section contains a list of comps that can be browsed by the client to explore a variety of interface options. The Design Manager or Project Manager places comps online for the client to examine and comment on. Typically there will be a facility for attaching comments to each comp, so clients can make comments for the designers to read.

This section may also contain design concepts for specific elements of the site such as buttons and headers, and designs for supporting material such as print advertising and banners.

Getting Started

>**Phase 1: Strategic Planning<**

Phase 2: Design And Engineering

Phase 3: Production

Phase 4: Launch / Promotion

Post-Launch: Running The Site

Endmatter

8. Objectives

Why do you want a website anyway?

For some reason many companies forget basic business practices in their haste to jump on the Internet bandwagon. As with any other aspect of your business, your Internet strategy should be formulated with a solid commitment to defined objectives as part of a business plan.

Without defined deliverables you will have a very hard time achieving a focus for your site and no way to measure its success. There has to be some clearly defined purpose for its existence, and this is always the first thing I attempt to determine when commencing a new site development project. If your site structure has links on the home page to "learn more about our directors", then that purpose is probably just executive ego enhancement – unless, of course, it's a prospectus site and you're about to float. There are always exceptions!

The phrase on everyone's lips should be "ROI" (Return On Investment).

The concept of ROI is that the end result must be worth the money, effort, and time you put in to achieve it.

It may be that the desired return is direct financial gain, which could be achieved by any one of the revenue models discussed in Chapter 10: *Revenue Models*. Maybe the desired return is increased brand awareness, which in itself does not provide an immediately measurable financial gain but benefits your business in the long term. Maybe you intend to make money by saving money, reducing your overheads in a particular area such as after-sales support. Or maybe the return will be increased familiarity with the Internet and the processes involved as a preliminary step in a long term plan.

Product sales

Sales can be made online in order to reach new markets, decrease transaction costs and increase convenience for your customers. Whether this is cost effective for your business depends largely on the profit margin, unit transaction cost and shipping issues. It may be worthwhile for some of your products but not others. It also depends on the receptivity of your market to online transactions. Some market segments show a high degree of acceptance and trust in online transactions and will readily order a product online. Others may be hesitant to buy online and would prefer to use the Internet for product research before performing the actual transaction off-line.

The unit value of the sale must be worthwhile. Selling a liter of milk to consumers would cost more per transaction than the unit sale, but a milk distributor taking orders from stores that order hundreds of liters at a time may be worthwhile. Of course this is also dependent on accepted practice for the industry - if all the other milk distributors have sales reps, store owners may resent what they see as a lack of personal service. On the other hand, they may appreciate the lower prices and the reduced number of reps peddling their wares during store busy periods.

Conversely, the unit value must not be so high that it exceeds the capabilities of the transaction systems in place on the Internet. If you work on an account basis you can feel free to sell supertankers and jumbo jets online if you wish, but few people have a credit card that will cover them for more than a couple of thousand dollars.

Lead generation

Lead generation is perhaps the most direct way that a business in a service industry can profit from a site, and may also be the most appropriate approach for those marketing customized or big ticket items. Merchandising companies, for example, must customize every sale to suit the specific requirements of each client, since all products are modified with the logo or other identifying mark of the client. In a situation like this your site can be used to generate leads which are then followed up on a more personal level via email, snail mail, fax, telephone or in person by a sales rep.

The whole purpose of a lead generation site is to have the prospective client contact you and then take the level of communication onto a more personal basis, so it is vitally important that you make your company as easily accessible as possible. Make sure your contact details are everywhere, with at least an email link on every page. Telephone and fax numbers (with international prefixes) and your postal address should be easily found on a contact page and the main page of your site. Personally I like to see this information on every page of a site, but if you don't go that far at least make it easy for people to find.

You may wish to include small photographs and email addresses of your sales staff to personalize them in the minds of those who have never met them face to face. don't take this too far, though. You just need to give a personal face to your organization, not give full page biographies of the directors.

Increased brand awareness

"Branding" means increasing brand recognition among your potential client base, and building an association between a product category and your specific product name. It's not something the Internet does well at all. However, there are ways it can be done: for example, if you build a resource that becomes popular and attracts a lot of traffic, having your company name associated with it will build awareness of your brand among it's users.

You can also use push-marketing techniques as discussed in Chapter 21: *Multi-Touch Marketing* to build awareness subsequent to the initial contact.

Reduced overheads

Put simply, the Internet can save you money. Lots of money. Many Internet projects could be financed out of the savings in printing and postage alone, with all the other benefits such as increased sales just icing on the cake. For example, one of my clients was spending $70,000 per year printing and distributing material-safety data sheets to their dealers. For a vastly smaller figure we converted all the data sheets into a format suitable for Internet access, and even had a thousand or so CDs pressed to be distributed to dealers needing off-line access. My client saved about $55,000/year and everyone was happy – except their printing company!

Whenever I hear someone say they can't find the budget for a website I ask them about the sort of information they send out during the course of a normal business week. This could include product data sheets, press releases, advertising brochures, internal memos, internal and external newsletters, product announcements, supplier orders, product designs, and much more. Obviously not everything is suited to electronic distribution, but just converting some of your organization's correspondence to electronic format could save large amounts of time, printing and postage.

Internet familiarity

Because integrating the Internet with your business requires such a different way of thinking, it's important to start somewhere and have something to build on. This doesn't mean undertaking a project you know will fail – it means doing the very best you can with the budget and resources you have available to you. As you work with the Internet your ideas will change, your expectations will mature, and you will be in a better position to make your website a success than someone who waited a while longer and put everything in place at the last moment.

Define the purpose

So grab a notebook and write down the specific objectives of your website. It may be vague now, but it will give you something to refine and help you brief your developer more accurately. Then once you have a few objectives noted down you can decide on relevant metrics by which to measure the success of the site: it could be unit or dollar sales from the site, or number of site visitors per month. Without measurability, you will have no way to determine the ROI you have achieved.

Web metrics and analytics: measuring success

Web metrics are the benchmarks by which the success of a website can be measured, and analytics is the process of measuring and reporting on whether a site achieves those metrics.

In the early days of the web all that mattered was how many "hits" your site received each month, but as I'll explain in Chapter 25: *Understanding Traffic Statistics* hits are a meaningless term for most purposes. Web metrics are now much more sophisticated and can be tuned to the specific objectives of your site. The type of site you run will determine what type of metrics you should set.

Retail (Business-To-Consumer) site metrics

If you are actually selling things online there are some reasonably straightforward metrics you can employ.

Nett dollars per visitor is an obvious measure, and one that can be very informative. Your website traffic analysis software (more about this in Chapter 25) should be able to give you a figure for the number of unique visitors who come to your site each month, day and week. By dividing the total value of orders received by the visitor count for that period you obtain a figure for nett dollars per visitor.

Drop-off rates are a measure of how many visitors to your site either leave without placing an order, or abandon a shopping cart after placing items in it. These two figures give you valuable information about whether users are following through with transactions on your site, or whether they have problems you need to investigate to decrease the drop-off rate.

Clickstream analysis is the process of investigating the sequence of pages that typical users follow on your site. It's really a more detailed version of drop-off rate measurement with a focus that goes down to items like which are the most common entry and exit pages on your site, and the path a typical user takes through the site.

Business-to-Business site metrics

Business-to-business (B2B) sites are very different to retail sites because they are usually focused on providing the smoothest and simplest supply-chain process possible without garnishing it with marketing frills. As a result the metrics that you want are often the exact opposite of a retail site. You don't want users spending huge amounts of time on the system and racking up massive page view counts, because that indicates the system is probably not very efficient at allowing them to find what they're looking for.

System performance is the measure of how fast pages can be served up to users. With a B2B site which will be accessed by impatient users it's critical to keep everything running as snappily as possible. One way to measure system performance would be to have a script that loads a page on your site every 5 minutes and measures how long it takes to be served up: measuring the page load time is an important way to track whether your site is keeping up with the load being placed on it. Substandard performance will drive users away.

Session duration is a measurement of how long each person spends on the site. While it sounds illogical, a B2B site should strive for the shortest average session duration possible while increasing the number of sessions. Many short sessions are an indicator that users are achieving their objectives on the site, especially if the ratio of sales to sessions is high.

Content / advertising site metrics

Sites which serve up content and make money from advertising revenues such as banner ads need to make sure they are reaching the right type of users in order to sell advertising.

Banner statistics are obviously critical to any site that bases its revenue on banners. The single most important figure is the CTR, or click-through rate: that is, what percentage of banner impressions result in a user clicking the banner. If there are 13 clicks for every 100 banners you display, your CTR is

13%. Very simple, but probably the single most important statistic for a banner-carrying site. You should measure the CTR for each banner individually so you know who your best (and worst) performers are.

Loyalty index is a measure of how many site visitors are regulars, returning on a daily, monthly or annual basis to the site. This can be tracked using long-term cookies which are set in the user's browser or by having users log in to the site with a username and password, with web analytics software generating a report showing the average number of visits each user makes within a specified period.

Customer satisfaction is one of the hardest things to measure: in fact, very few site operators even try it. Traffic statistics will tell you what site visitors do but it won't tell you how they feel. Many sites resort to visitor surveys to collect satisfaction data, often placing site visitors in a prize draw in exchange for completing the survey. Without a nice carrot as encouragement not many users will bother completing a survey form!

Web metrics and analytics is a field that has grown considerably in sophistication in the last couple of years, with many web developers now building statistical reporting tools directly into site management systems. Even if the Content Management System that runs your site can't generate web analytics reports you can still generate reports using third-party tools, including software that processes your server log
files as well as external analytics providers who track your site users on your behalf.

One of the most popular systems recently has been Google Analytics, which allows you to generate very detailed visitor behavior reports simply by adding a small snippet of code to each page of your website.

More details of Google Analytics is available at www.google.com/analytics.

9. Your Target Demographic
Who do you think you're talking to?

Now you've documented the objectives for your website (you've done that, haven't you?) the next thing to do is define who you want to make use of your site. In marketing terms this is known as defining the target demographic profile and then, based on that, the target psychographic profile. Ask yourself a few general questions like:

- What experience do my potential clients have with the Internet?
- What is their income?
- What are their interests?
- How old are they?
- Are they repeat customers or once-only sales?

There are many questions like these which will help you broadly define the kind of person you want to reach. Also ask yourself a few questions more specifically related to your business to help you define your particular target market. For example, if you are developing a travel or destination site:

- Do my potential clients travel often?
- Who do they travel with?
- Do they stay long?
- What are their other interests?
- Are they easily mobile?

Personalize the market

The procedure above is probably familiar to anyone with a marketing background and it's the way things have been done for many years. It's common to see marketing plans with nicely defined target demographics, but in my opinion that doesn't take things nearly far enough.

You don't do business with a customer category, you do business with a whole range of individuals. At the end of the day, your customers are people just like you – even if you sell to corporate clients, they aren't the real customer. It's the person within that corporation that matters.

We're all human, and you need to be able to think of your customers that way.

Creating demographic profiles

Define a number of hypothetical people who are representative of your target market. They may be based on actual people you deal with every day, they may be a composite of a number of real customers, or as a last resort they may be totally fictional.

For example, an inner city beautician might define her target demographic as including "Sally, 19 years old, a school leaver in her first year of full time work for a large firm. She has few commitments, a moderate income and focuses on her image amongst her peers and workmates". A fishing tackle supplier in a seaside resort might define their target demographic as including "Bob, 43 years old, married with 3 kids. He has financial and family commitments and focuses on maximum quality of life".

These sorts of profiles may seem simplistic compared to the nicely formatted tables and graphs of a traditional demographic definition, but they will start you thinking along the right track. Imagine Sally or Bob as a real person, someone you meet in the street and have a conversation with. What are their hobbies? What are they interested in? Who do they spend time with? What do they do for recreation? What are their worries and fears? And how comfortable are they with the Internet?

Many companies have several different types of customers so create an imaginary profile to represent each one. A paint shop may have customers including young couples renovating their first home, professional painters, and retired people doing routine home maintenance – each has quite distinct traits and levels of experience, and therefore very different expectations and requirements.

Imagine each of your hypothetical characters as a real person with real requirements and pressures. If they were talking to you directly rather than looking at your website, what questions would they ask you? What would you chat about? How could you best help them achieve their personal objectives?

Now imagine them sitting down in front of a computer and looking at your website. They are the same person and their needs haven't changed, but now they are limited to dealing with you via the web. What are they going to look for? How can you answer their questions and provide them personal service when they aren't standing in front of you?

By personalizing each customer group in this way you can better understand how to service them, and define the sorts of things you will need to put on your website.

It may feel childish but make a couple of copies of **Appendix D**: *User Profile*

Worksheet and take the time to write up some profiles. It's a simple step but accurately defining your users will form the basis of subsequent site planning. Your developer will thank you for it.

Beyond demographics: psychographics

The demographic profiling I have just explained is primarily concerned with defining *who* your clients and potential clients are, that is, defining marketplace reality. Even if you stop at that point you'll be way ahead of most businesses, but you can take it a step further by developing psychographic profiles as well.

Psychographic profiling is a matter of defining *why* people within your target demographic make buying decisions, that is, *perceived* marketplace reality. Psychographic techniques involve defining the conscious and subconscious needs of your target demographic. These are the real reasons they buy or don't buy – and they probably have nothing whatsoever to do with what they are buying. It's much more low-level than that, usually below the level of conscious rationalization. It's at the gut level where they decide whether they can identify with you, whether they can trust you, and whether they want to do business with you. It may sound airy-fairy, but customer psychographics are an incredibly powerful force that can help you or hurt you at all levels of your business.

By way of illustration, think about the last time you bought a hamburger. Are you in the habit of going to a big franchise or do you prefer to buy burgers from a small Ma-n-Pa shop? If you were in a new town you hadn't visited before and were faced with both a familiar burger franchise and a Ma-n-Pa burger shop right next to each other, which would you walk into? If they were being honest, most people would say the franchise. Now ask yourself which one you would expect to produce a tastier burger: most people would probably say the Ma-n-Pa shop.

Why is that? Why do franchise burger chains get all the business, when most people think little local shops do a better job of making tasty burgers?

The answer is revealed by examining the difference in psychographic profiles of typical customers of the two businesses and how those differences influence the purchasing decision. The franchise chain is fulfilling emotional needs that customers probably aren't even aware of, such as expectations of consistency, hygiene, and value. The little local shop is merely fulfilling the need for tasty burgers, not realizing that when it comes to a burger purchasing decision most people subconsciously put the quality of the actual product way down the list of priorities.

Understanding the critical question of why people *really* make a purchasing decision is what psychographic profiling is all about. It's a complex field that I won't explain in detail here, but hopefully this introduction has given you enough food for thought as a starting point.

Beyond psychographics: behavior analysis

So demographics is about defining *who* your target customers are, and psychographics is about *why* those people do things. Even if you're starting out a brand new business with no trading history you can probably take a pretty good stab at predicting both those attributes, and even a guess is better than nothing.

Behavior analysis, on the other hand, is about measuring *what* people do. You can't guess it or predict it: you can only measure it. It's about not letting yourself be blindsided by the marketplace as a result of focusing on theoretical models rather than measuring what people actually do.

Think about it this way. Your business has a particular product or service to sell. You might have a carefully thought out business plan with customer demographic profiles which show your target market is 40 to 60 year old married women, but if a teenage boy walks in the door and plunks down some cash and says "give me two of those" are you going to tell him to get lost just because he doesn't fit the profile? Of course not. Maybe you won't be geared up to serve him as effectively as someone who does fit your target demographic profile, but the important thing is not whether potential customers fit your that profile: it's whether they fit the *behavior* pattern of people you are trying to reach.

Right now you're probably thinking "Did I really need to read a book to be told that people who buy from me are my customers? And if all I have to care about is what people do, why do I have to bother with demographic and psychographic profiling?"

The answer to both those questions is part of the critical next step, a mental leap that few business operators make: when behavior of a customer changes in any way it should make you sit bolt upright with your eyes wide open and say "what the hell just happened?"

If a customer visits your website every day to read the news headlines and then suddenly stops, what happened? Maybe she found a more relevant news service.

If a customer orders a pizza from your online pizza delivery service every 2 weeks or so and then one day the orders stop, what happened? Maybe he found cheaper pizza.

The change can be in a positive direction, too. If someone has been receiving your email newsletter for years and then one day places an order with you, what happened? The relationship between you went to the next level, that's what. Time to start treating them differently to all the other random subscribers to your newsletter.

The above examples indicate behavioral deviation of an individual from the previous behavior of that particular individual. Behavioral deviation can also be examined relative to a statistical group. For example, maybe 91% of your new customers contact your technical support line between 2 and 4 times within the first year and only 4% call 5 or more times. Then one customer places their 6th call after being with you for just 2 months. Once again, you should ask yourself "what just happened?"

Events like this should cause an alarm to go off that causes you to examine the situation in more detail and react appropriately to the needs of the particular customer.

The big problem is that most of the time we're too busy getting on with business to notice these changes. It's not even a blip on the radar when a customer stops calling you, until one day you come across something that reminds you of them and you suddenly realize you haven't heard from them in over a year.

But by then it's too late. They're not your customer any more. They're someone else's.

By measuring and analyzing customer behavior you can "red flag" such changes, allowing you to pro-actively seek feedback from them so you can understand the change and then act on what you learn. Ideally this process should be automated: for example, if your tech support staff use a CRM (Customer Relationship Management) system to record all incoming calls it would be a simple matter to have the system raise an alert if any customer calls more than X times in Y days. These triggers (or "tripwires") allow you to define expected normal parameters for customer behavior and then minimize the number of customers who slip through the cracks because their behavior changes go unnoticed.

One of the most interesting writers in this field is Jim Novo, who has written a number of useful books including *Drilling Down: Turning Customer Data Into Profits With A Spreadsheet.* Jim does a great job of explaining the concepts in simple terms and then showing how to implement basic behavior tripwires using readily available tools. You can find out more on his site at www.jimnovo.com.

10. Revenue Models
Show me the money!

If you actually did the exercises in the last chapter and have some user profiles defined, you'll now have at least some basis for defining your revenue model.

Most websites are developed for a specific purpose - to make money. Planning in advance exactly how you intend to do so is a very important step. Putting product information on the web is not enough. You need to think through what you intend users to do once they have access to that info: do you want them to order online? Or maybe visit an off-line retail outlet? Phone or mail an order through?

Maybe you're planning to make money by providing information online and charging for access to it, or placing paid advertising on your site. Whatever your revenue model, you must plan it.

Online sales

This revenue model can be a direct extension of your current sales channel. If you have a product that can be packaged and shipped, you can sell it from your website. If your products are standardized you can take credit card details online then have the transaction authorized automatically in real time by your bank and have a shipping order sent to your warehouse staff for fulfillment. The bank transfers the funds directly into your account, and the sale is completed.

Software products can be sold online in downloadable form with users paying to download it from your server. Some software companies now sell entirely by online distribution and don't even have to copy and box their software anymore. They can sell 10 copies or 10,000 for almost the same cost. And they never have to worry about producing too much stock and having it made obsolete by a new version.

Other businesses dealing in Internet-delivered products include image galleries for designers, record companies who charge to download music files, and virtual publishers who charge to access books and documents.

If your products are customized you can use a form that takes the specific details from the customer and forwards them to you as an email so you can quote on the job.

Referral income

Referral income is royalties from companies to whom you refer potential customers. Affiliate or associate programs work in this manner. They pay per click-through, per action, or as a percentage of any sales that result from the referral. Income can vary from 5 cents to $1.00 per click-through, or from 5% to 20% of sales. The great grand-daddy affiliate program of them all was created by Amazon.com, which has over 900,000 affiliate websites.

Content fees

Fees may be charged if you have something on your site that people are willing to pay to access. This could include content for business, entertainment, or educational purposes.

An important factor to consider for fee based information sites is the transaction cost - the technology for micro-payments (payments in the region of fractions of a cent up to a few cents) is coming, but it is not here yet. So it's not yet practical to have an online newspaper that charges a tiny amount per article. However, if you can provide a service that will entice visitors to pay a subscription fee you may be able to generate substantial revenue by charging for content.

A number of sites offer compelling content for business such as research reports or access to online databases, or even regular feature articles in a particular field. This can be a hard area to compete in due to the strong tradition of freedom of information on the Internet. It's very likely that information being sold on one site for a substantial sum is made freely available on other sites. One successful subscription-based online business resource is The Wall Street Journal at www.wsj.com.

Subscription based entertainment has been largely dominated in the past by porn sites, but the subscription revenue model is now extending to many other forms of entertainment. Some multi-player online games offer a free trial and then monthly subscriptions to play indefinitely. I expect that a lot of high-value, time critical content will move to subscription or pay-per-view models in the next couple of years.

Advertising

Banner advertising, when used as a revenue stream, is charging other people to place their banner ads on your site. Visitors then see the banners on your site and can click on them to go to the advertiser's site.

I don't generally recommend the use of banner advertising as a revenue stream to my clients because it tends to dilute their message and distract the user from the primary purpose of the site. If you have a site that is attracting a number of potential customers it makes no sense to present banners that may catch their attention, draw them away from your site and perhaps lose yourself a sale all for the sake of a few cents of advertising revenue.

But if your site has significant traffic that does not directly benefit your business, advertising may turn an operating expense into a revenue stream. For example, you may have a site that offers a free public service and does not generate money, but has a large number of targeted visitors (that is, visitors with a specific common interest such as a hobby).

Banners are generally sold in units called CPM, or cost per thousand impressions. Typical CPMs vary from US$5 to $70 depending on how tightly targeted the visitors are. The more tightly targeted they are, the more accurately you can define their interests and therefore the more you can charge to relevant advertisers. CPMs have been gradually declining over the last couple of years, and sites selling banner space are having trouble getting buyers even at reduced rates.

Banner advertising is not likely to make you much money on its own. If you had tightly targeted traffic of 10,000 page views (not hits) per month and charged $20 CPM, you would make $200 / month. Not very impressive, considering the effort of creating content that will attract 10,000 page views per month. On the other hand, if you run a major portal site that handles traffic of millions of users a month you may find that advertising revenue could significantly offset your running costs.

When selling banner advertising, your "inventory" is the number of page views that your site has available for banners. With so many sites now selling banner space you may have trouble selling enough banners to fill the inventory. You then need to fill the rest of the page views each month with uncharged banners, such as banners advertising your own services. Make sure you factor in a realistic sale rate when calculating expected income. The example above of 10,000 page views per month generating $200 income is assuming a 100% sale of inventory: if the site owner could only sell 50% of the inventory, they'd be making just $100 per month from it.

Another banner revenue model which has grown in popularity is pay-per-click, or PPC. That is, you carry a banner for an advertiser who pays you nothing unless a visitor clicks on the ad. This model is preferred by advertisers because they don't have to pay anything up front and they only pay if the ad works. It's disliked by site owners for exactly the same reason. The site owner has no control over ad quality - an advertiser may saddle them with a poorly designed banner that generates almost no click-throughs, when the site owner could be making more money with another advertiser whose banners generate lots of clicks and sales.

11. Site Structure And Focus
Drawing up the plans

Now you know what the purpose of your site is going to be, who will use it, and what you want them to do. Next you need to pull all that together into a planned structure.

This is where things really start to come together and your developer should drive this stage of the process quite actively through the direct involvement of their Information Architect if they have one. Many smaller web development business get by without a specialist Information Architect, with the role typically falling on the Project Manager and / or Account Executive.

To help you understand what's going on and work productively with your developer I'll cover a few of the issues that are likely to come up at this stage.

Domain name

Selection of a domain name has a few things to consider, including trademarks, guessability, memorability, phonetics, length, and relevance to your customers.

It's very important to make sure your domain name does not contravene anyone's trademark or service mark. Otherwise you could find yourself in hot water if they decide to appeal to the domain registration authorities or even take action in court.

Guessability allows people to go through a quick mental "what if?" to come up with your URL. For example, I may meet someone and tell them I'm from a company called "IVT". Later they want to check out the IVT site, so they think "hmm, I'll take the name and put 'www' in front, so now I've got 'www.ivt', then I'll add a 'com', but they're an Australian company so I'll add 'au' as well, so I think the address must be 'www.ivt.com.au'."

Bingo, they've got the domain.

Note that people won't actually make much effort at this, and they won't try lots of different extensions. Many people will try one guess using an extension like 'com' (or 'com.au' for example if they are somewhere like Australia) but if that fails, they'll give up. They probably won't try guessing with more obscure extensions like 'net.au', 'org', or 'cc' so try to use the dominant extension for your region, whatever that may be.

Memorability is an important issue because most people aren't very good at remembering URLs. Most people have trouble just remembering the name of a person they met five minutes ago, so how are they going to remember your URL if they see it flashed up on the side of a bus for three seconds? Will they be able to recall it an hour later at home in front of their computer? This is another reason that you should try to use a standard domain extension if you possibly can. People may just remember the significant portion of your name, but not the extension. Then they'll go through the guessing process above to try to extrapolate the rest.

The phonetics of the domain is very important. Think about how the URL will sound when spoken. I have seen many attempts to create clever URLs that become almost impossible to speak in an unambiguous way, even if they make perfect sense when written down. Be particularly careful of numbers in a URL because I can guarantee it'll have to be explained every single time. "Check out www.hair4you.com ... no, it's 'four', not 'F O R' ... no, the actual number 4". Confusion city.

This goes double for the words 'dot' and 'com'. Never include them in a URL - how do you say 'www.mynamedotcom.com' without confusing someone? Depending on their understanding of how domains work, they could misinterpret this as 'www.myname.com.com', 'www.mynamedotcomdotcom', 'www.myname.comdotcom', and various other permutations. When you say 'dot' it has to mean '.', and nothing else. Of course, there are always exceptions and some people actually get away with it - like 'www.dot.com', and the venerable 'slashdot.org' where the domain has become the brand.

slashdot.org: Defying domain name common sense, but in this case it works. Don't try this at home, kids.

Relevance to your customers is really a question of what name they know you by. If they know you by the branding of your product range, it may not make sense to use a domain based on your actual company name: it probably makes more sense to base it on your product branding instead. If a girl was looking online for information about Barbie dolls do you think she'd open up a browser and try www.mattel.com? Not likely! The first guess would be www.barbie.com every time.

When choosing a domain you should do a simple test: tell a couple of people your brand name (company or product, as appropriate) and ask them to guess your website address. This is actually a very good way to come up with a quick answer to what domain you should use. Then tell a couple of people the address orally and ask them to write it down. If they need you to clarify the spelling in order to get it right, the domain may still be too ambiguous phonetically.

As for length, shorter is better. 'Nuff said.

The magic number 7

How many items can a person retain in short term memory, allowing them to read a list of options through once and make a selection without re-reading the list? Psychologist George Miller performed studies way back in the 1950s which showed the typical person has a short term memory capable of retaining 7(+/-2) items. That is, between 5 and 9. As a result 7(+/- 2) has become known as the magic number of interface design, the sweet spot at which the designer can present as many options as possible without confusing site visitors. Most site designers therefore aim to structure site navigation around providing 7(+/- 2) options at any one time.

While that's a very useful rule of thumb, things aren't actually quite that simple and there are times when it may be valid to present more than 7 options to a site visitor. A news site, for example, may list several dozen news headlines on the home page. What's most important is to strike a balance so the site doesn't present too many options to a user at once, and conversely doesn't make them go through 500 levels of menus with very few options in each just to get to where they need to be.

For an example of why too many options are bad take a look at the screenshot on the next page. It's the home page of a certain very well known site, and believe it or not it has 298 links and 9 forms on it! The developers have attempted to structure the page with multiple link hierarchies such as bold headings to aid comprehension, but even understanding the hierarchy takes several seconds of examination. A quick count shows 7 different levels in the hierarchy. This is made worse by the fact that even on a very large monitor it's not possible to see even half of the items at once. Believe it or not this page is a big improvement on the previous version which was almost totally incomprehensible. I've been using that page as an example of how not to do site navigation for years, and I've been living in constant fear that one day they'll redesign the site and I'll lose my favorite example.

Non-linear information

Websites should be structured so they can be accessed in a non-linear way. Linear access is when information is accessed by starting at the beginning and moving to the end, such as in a novel. With non-linear access, a visitor may begin at any page and progress to any other, following an unpredictable path, more like a reference book. While your site may be designed to nicely guide the visitor through a series of pages if they start at the beginning or "home" page, many visitors will enter your site from a search engine or link that may direct them straight to a page deep inside the site.

It's therefore extremely important that a new user can enter your site at any page and still gain an understanding of the overall context as well as how to get to other parts of the site. Something I still see from time to time is pages that have no navigation links whatsoever, so that if you get to them from outside the site (such as from a search engine) there is

no simple way to get to the rest of the site. Developers sometimes call this phenomenon "pages from outer space" because when you get there you have no idea what their context is or how to go elsewhere.

Levels of navigation

Having arrived at your site visitors will rely on the site navigation to assist and direct them to the information or page they want. A typical site consists of many pages of content, and some sites have millions of pages. It's vitally important that visitors can see where they are within the overall hierarchy of the site, and figure out both how they got there and how to move to other areas.

This is usually done by breaking the site into an upside-down tree structure with the home page at the top. Below that a number of major sections will be defined, and the home page will have links into those sections. This is known as first-tier, or top-level, navigation. Each of those sections may then diverge to many other pages or sub sections, known as second-tier navigation. To provide context for visitors it's usual to provide links to all top-level sections on all pages, allowing visitors to quickly move to an area of interest from anywhere in the site.

So the first thing to do is decide on the major sections of the site for the first-tier navigation. Remember that magic number I mentioned earlier? This is where site designers use it. As a general rule you should try to have no more than about 7(+/- 2) first-tier sections in your site, or visitors will get confused and take longer to make a decision about which one to enter.

Keep in mind that this is just a guideline and there may be valid reasons to break your site up further. However, if you have a requirement for many top-level sections you may need to rethink your structure, or perhaps even spin off sub-sites dedicated to specific business areas, divisions or products. Sony, for example, has widely diverging product streams - go to www.sony.com and you will see links to sub-sites dedicated to specific markets, such as Music, Electronics, Playstation, etc. Each Sony sub-site is totally different, with its own look, color scheme, and structure to suit its particular market. If this is the case for your business, you should treat each sub-site as a separate project. Go through the entire process of defining objectives, a target market, site structure etc for each one. What may work for one market or product line may not work for another.

Site maps

Once your site content has been "chunked" into bite-size pieces it can be very helpful to draw up a site map. A site map is a bit like a flowchart that shows how the different sections of the site link together, and provides a visual overview of at least the major sections of the site. On small sites it could even list every single page on the site, but most modern sites have way too much content to be able to represent every page individually in a site map. The critical thing is to represent the overall structure of the site with the different sections defined within each level of navigation.

Some Content Management Systems have the ability to create a site map automatically from an existing site, allowing you to put a site map directly on your site so users can access it to find their way around. That can be a great idea if your site is complex, but it doesn't help during the planning stages because you can't generate the map until pages and sections have already been added to the CMS. An automatically generated site map is a bit like the "You are here" maps you find inside the entrances to shopping centers: fantastic for visitors once the shopping center has been built, but not much use to the engineers responsible for building it in the first place. What they need are blueprints to show them where everything needs to go, and likewise the site map created by your Information Architect during the strategic planning phase will later be used by your developer to put all your content in the correct place.

Depth of information

How much information should you present to visitors about your products and services? Do you just provide a one-sentence summary and a "buy now" button, or do you provide a 200 page technical review, a 3D virtual reality model, customer testimonials and a try-before-you-buy simulation?

It all comes down to how much information it takes to satisfy a purchaser that they have made the correct product selection, without providing so much information that they go into data overload. This is a matter of analyzing where your sales sit on the scale of high-consideration versus low-consideration transactions.

Whether a transaction is high or low consideration depends on a number of factors:

- Initial transaction cost
- Total cost of ownership (ongoing expenses)
- Expected period of ownership / use
- Emotional link between item and personal identity (ego)
- The potential impact of a wrong choice

The easiest way to understand this is to look at some extreme examples.

Purchase of a new car would generally be considered a high-consideration transaction. The purchase value is significant, the total cost of ownership is high, the expected period of ownership extends over several years and many people emotionally link their self-image and therefore ego to their car. Many people feel that others will, rightly or wrongly, judge their worth as a person on what they drive. Those factors add up to a transaction where the purchaser will usually want a lot of information and reassurance prior to the sale.

Purchase of a bottle of milk would generally be low-consideration – purchase price is low, cost of ownership is nil (other than refrigeration), period of ownership is hours or days, and emotional link is low. Not many people judge others on what brand of milk they buy!

Of course it isn't possible to fix a type of transaction on a scale identically for every person. A lactose-intolerant fleet manager for a large company may not think twice about buying a new car because they do it every day, but purchase of a carton of milk could be a high-consideration transaction for that person.

Call to action

Once you have convinced the site visitor to use your product or service you need to tell them what to do next. In marketing terms, this step is known as the "Call To Action". The call to action is how you direct the visitor to respond to what they see on the site, and therefore how you want to close the sale.

You may have heard marketing advice like "always be closing", which means to always be guiding the visitor to complete the transaction. Don't put barriers between your visitors and a sale: it may be important to provide a detailed, step by step tour of the product to reassure new customers, but if they have to go all the way through the tour before they can complete the transaction it may become a barrier. Make sure that at any point they can complete the transaction if they have made a decision. A guided product tour, for example, may have 15 steps, but if you place a call to action such as a "Buy Now" link on every page of the tour a visitor can reach step 7 and complete the purchase without going through the rest of the tour.

So considering each section or page of your site, think about what you want the user to do next. Do you want them to purchase online? Contact a dealer? Contact your sales staff for off-line follow-up? This is your call to action for that section or page, so make it easy for the visitor to do it.

Balance this out against appearing too pushy to make a sale. The visitor should be able to obtain enough information from your site to make a decision, and having arrived at that decision it should be totally painless to take the next step of completing the transaction. The option to complete the transaction should always be there, but without being so overbearing that the visitor feels they are having a hard-sell routine shoved down their throat.

12. The Design Brief
Designing the user experience

One of the most difficult tasks faced by web developers is guiding clients through the early stages of the design phase. Developing a design or "look" for a website needs to take many factors into account, such as:

- Existing corporate image definition including logo and corporate colors.
- The structure or "flow" of the site.
- The profile of a typical user.
- The technologies deemed appropriate for the project such as Flash and DHTML.

With constraints like these in mind a site designer's worst nightmare is a client who says "I don't know what I want it to look like, but I'll know it when I see it." In that situation the designer can create random design concepts until the cows come home and still never strike upon something the client approves.

The way to keep this stage on track is to develop a "design brief", and this is where all the information collated during Phase 1 (Strategic Planning) really starts to become useful. Many people think that creating a design is all about sitting around until inspiration strikes, and that it's a very poorly defined and illogical process. However, as any professional designer will tell you there are very will refined processes used to end up with a good design, and the process is more of a logical sequence than you may realize.

My company uses a worksheet to help our clients think through this process in a logical way. You can find an example worksheet in Appendix E: *Design Brief Worksheet*.

It's very important to keep in mind through this stage is that websites are all about content: the purpose of the design is not to dazzle the site visitor, but to help them find and comprehend the content. Don't let all the design options distract you from the actual purpose of your site!

Corporate colors and logo

One of the most fundamental issues with design of a typical corporate website is that it should comply with the standard "look" of the organization. Companies generally have a standard corporate identity, but the formality of that identity may vary dramatically.

For example, your company may have a logo, a letterhead and a business card design but that's about it. Anyone within the organization may have the freedom to format other material as they see fit.

On the other extreme, your company may have a very formally defined corporate image that goes to the extent of documenting what fonts may be used in various internal and external communication, how letters should be formatted, the size and location of the logo in relation to other elements on a page, how the telephone should be answered, and what music you have "on hold" on your telephones. Some companies, such as Apple Computer, go so far as to have custom fonts designed and require those fonts be used in specific circumstances, and explicitly not used elsewhere. This is all part of controlling the "experience" of coming into contact with the company and ensuring a consistent image is portrayed.

All of this information is priceless to your web developer.

Existing marketing material

Along with the corporate image definition you should provide as much collateral material as possible. This can include brochures, product data sheets, posters, television spots, etc. It all helps the designer get a sense of context and a feel for how your organization should be portrayed, even if the material itself is not used directly.

> **Mood Colors:** Designers have long understood that colors can evoke emotional responses. When used in combination certain colors can give site visitors very different impressions.
>
> For example, orange gives the impression of being dynamic, blue is associated with trustworthiness, and green invokes impressions of wealth.
>
> Large companies deliberately exploit these associations as part of their image management strategy: IBM didn't gain the nickname "Big Blue" by chance.

There may also need to be tie-ins with marketing in other media, such as a brochure that directs customers to a special offer on your website. It's important for your various media to be tightly coordinated to prevent bad experiences for customers, such as entering a URL from a catalog and getting an error like "page not found".

I've seen some big mistakes: one client took out expensive magazine advertising without double-checking their site address, and didn't realize they'd put in the wrong domain name until people started phoning to complain that the URL in the ad didn't work! Then the client called me in a panic to see if the domain they had listed in the ad could be registered in a hurry since it was too late to fix the ad itself. Doh!

Reference sites

One of the best ways to get your brain moving in the right direction is to critique existing sites that you like. Spend time on the Internet looking at the sites of your suppliers, your clients, your competitors, or any other random thing you come across. They don't have to be in your industry – don't limit yourself at this point.

As you are looking at these sites, ask yourself what you like and don't like about how they look. What colors provide the right mood and readability? Is the content cluttered or open? Where is the navigation located? Does the site convey a consistent image across multiple pages and sections?

Narrow the list down to 3 to 5 sites that have design elements you like, and write down the URLs along with a couple of sentences explaining exactly what you like or don't like about each design. Don't just give your designer a list of URLs and make them guess!

Site structure

One of the tasks of the site interface is to provide users with a sense of context so they can move confidently from page to page while understanding where they are and where they are going.

Your site designer will need to know what navigational cues should be visible to users in order to provide this feedback. This will probably include headers on each page that change depending on the section of the site the user is looking at. It may also determine how the first and second level navigation is designed.

While you should strive for internal consistency where possible, in the case of very large sites it may be appropriate to create a number of internal "sub-sites" with their own variation on the overall look and feel. This can allow different sections to have their own navigational structure and page layout optimized for that particular section.

Revenue model

If your website revenue model is going to include advertising revenue from paid or affiliate banners or links, make sure your interface designer knows how this will affect the layout. Banner dimensions need to be defined and allowed for in the page layout.

Target demographic

Back in Chapter 9: *Your Target Demographic*, we went through the process of defining who will be using your site. A number of hypothetical "characters" were defined to assist with role-playing the activities of a typical site user. Pass this information on to your interface designer, because it will be very important in setting the design tone of the site: formal or informal, corporate or casual.

Technical requirements

Designing for the web has some distinct restrictions that may vary depending on what technical requirements are considered appropriate for your site. The starting point is basic HTML, which allows your designer to perform standard page layout. Additional design features such as page transitions, animation, sound, movies, sliding menus and objects, etc may require use of technologies such as Flash, DHTML (dynamic HTML), QuickTime, Java or Javascript.

The more technologies that are available to the designer the greater flexibility they will have in creating specific effects, but at a great trade-off: many users may not be able to use the site at all unless they have a specific browser version or a special "plug-in" that adds special features to the browser. Anything that puts a barrier between users and your site must be justified – remember that if using your site is too hard for users, your competitors are just a click away!

A decision on the base technical standard for the site will enable your interface designer to work within the constraints of the approved technologies.

13. Design Concepts And Drafts
What do you want it to look like?

Design concepts for the overall look and feel of the site (variously referred to as the "face", "front end", "interface", or "skin") are developed in a process known as "comping". Comping, an abbreviation of compositing, is a process of stitching together various images and original artwork to create a standard layout for the pages of the site. The result is often referred to as a "comp" or a "concept".

Comps should take into account all the factors discussed in Chapter 12: *The Design Brief* including established corporate colors and logo, design of existing and future advertising material, typical user profile, and the purpose of the site. It should also include navigation elements such as buttons or image maps. The navigation elements may not be final (it's common for designers to put dummy labels like "item 1", "item 2", etc on them in the early stages) but it's important to include them in the comp as they are intrinsically linked to the look of the site. In Chapter 11: *Site Structure And Focus* we covered site structure – at this point the site structure diagram will be used to determine what navigation needs to be visible at all times, and what appears only in specific contexts.

Initial design comps

Throughout the design process there won't be a single line of HTML written: everything is done as layered images that allow individual objects in the image to be moved and edited with relative ease. The most common tools for this are programs like Adobe PhotoShop and the GIMP (Gnu Image Manipulation Program).

The layered images are "flattened" into GIF or JPEG format images which are then presented to the client. Comps are not functional, so none of the links on them will work: they are just a single big image that is almost like a screenshot of what the site will look like. Dynamic objects like mouse-overs (buttons that change when the cursor is over them) and current-state buttons (buttons that look different to indicate that the user is in that section) will be displayed in an unchanging state.

When starting a new project we go through an internal brainstorming and trial design phase based on the design brief and any supporting material supplied by the client. Then we distill the ideas into about 3 different initial design comps, and present these comps to the client either at a meeting or by placing them online so they can be accessed with a web browser. Our extranet has a section specifically for design comps, allowing our clients to log into a password-protected area and review them.

These initial comps become the starting point for discussing specific design elements and overall layout with the client.

Design review process

Once the designs have been presented to the client we allow them to spend time reviewing the comps and making comments on them. At this point it is the job of your Site Manager to compile feedback for your developer's Design Manager or Project Manager. This is often done by discussing the designs over the phone or at a design review meeting. To make the review process as convenient as possible, our extranet also has a form under each design comp so the client can submit comments online.

Rather than rush through all this in one meeting we try to make it a three-step process: we present the designs, then give the client time to review them, then discuss their impressions and receive feedback. While initial reactions may be expressed at the design presentation, it's important to take the time to go over the designs at your leisure before going back to the developer with concise feedback. There may be a lot of detail to digest and you may also need to review design explanations the developer has provided before making a decision. It's no good to respond too fast and have the developer commence the next stage of development only to discover there is a flaw in the basic concept and you have to start again from scratch.

The final design

Having gone through the process of developing an interface design based on your feedback your developer will produce a candidate "final design". Right up to this point the design will still be in a layered format such as a Photoshop file, and presented to you as a static image such as a GIF or JPEG.

At this point you should know in a fair degree of detail what the site will look like. Colors will be final, page layout will be set, navigation will have been decided, font decisions made. Be sure that what you see (and approve) is what you really want. Changes later will be at your expense.

Image slicing

This is the point of design commitment, the time that it goes from being an easily modified concept to a complex system of images and HTML. Because comps are saved with all the different elements (buttons, headers, images, etc) in different layers it's simple to move things around and fine-tune the overall look. Once the layout has been finalized, the layers are "flattened" (merged into one) and the position of all elements is set permanently. The resulting design is then divided into smaller sections a bit like puzzle pieces. The pieces are then placed on the page using special tags in HTML and CSS (Cascading Style Sheet) files which define the location and relationship of various objects on each page.

From that point on changes to individual elements may still be reasonably simple, but larger changes (moving items around, changing colors, etc) may be considerably more difficult. It is very important to put the design through a rigorous assessment process before this point. Once a design is signed off changes become much more difficult.

14. Back-End Engineering
Dynamic websites: database magic

Databases are the sort of thing that leave many people scratching their heads asking what they actually do, but once you grasp the concepts and start applying database technology to your website a whole range of amazing possibilities open up.

But to understand how databases fit into the big picture you first need to understand how website content can be separated from design.

Content, functionality and interface

To display a web page your browser needs to be given a page that includes "tags" to describe the layout, and text and images for the content. The traditional way to create a website is to work out in advance exactly what pages will be required and what content will be displayed on each, and then create an HTML file for every page. So if you want a page for product A, you create an HTML file for that product. If you want a page for product B, you create another HTML file for that product as well. If you have 5,000 products, you create 5,000 pages. Then the pages are placed on a web server and away you go.

"So what?", you say, "That's the way websites are normally created."

OK, now think about this: what if your phone number changes, and it's displayed on every page of your site? Or worse still, what if you need to do a price rise of 4% on every single product? Oops, now you have to edit 5,000 pages by hand. Damn. Time to go and boil a very big pot of coffee!

The alternative is to divide your site into three logical parts:

The **content**: stored in a database that lives on your server and contains details of all the products, news items, articles, reviews etc you will have on your site.

The **functionality**: special software (often referred to as the "application layer" or "middleware") that takes content from the database and merges it with a template to create an HTML page on demand.

The **interface**: a page template without any specific information in it, just spaces where the content will be displayed. At my company we call this the "skin" of the site, and store it separately from the content and functionality so we can make a site look totally different by just "re-skinning" it.

With a system like this you don't need to create a page for every product. In fact, pages don't even need to exist on the server until the moment a web browser asks for them. When it receives a request the server runs the software in the function layer, which in turn accesses a database to retrieve the requested content, then mashes it into the template and sends it out as a complete HTML page to the visitor.

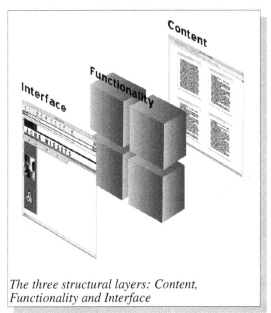

The three structural layers: Content, Functionality and Interface

Need to change your phone number? No problem, make one change to the template and every page viewed from then on will have the new details. Price update? Easy, do a bulk update on the database.

Right now you may still not quite see how powerful it can be to run your site from a database. In fact, what you've just read may seem like total gibberish and you don't have a clue what I'm talking about.

Don't worry, you're not alone. This is one of those concepts that can seem totally incomprehensible until you "get" it, but when the light bulb goes on it's definitely worth it.

The best way to get your head around the idea is to see it in action, so I've created a basic online demonstration that you can try live. Just go to www.stay-sane.com/dynamicsites and try it for yourself, then come back here for the rest of the chapter. Trust me, it's definitely worth taking the time to understand the concept.

So what can a site database do?

There are all sorts of things you can store in a site database, reaping the benefit of simple updates, visitor customization and data mining.

News. Keeping your site up to date with small, regular news snippets is a good low-effort way to indicate to your visitors that your site isn't stagnating in a corner. Store news items in a database to make them easily searchable and, perhaps more importantly, easy to update. Just make sure you put up news that's genuinely of interest to your customers – they probably couldn't care less about internal company events, but items such as product releases that provide them direct benefit can get their attention.

Products. The obvious thing to store in your site database for simple updates is product information. Product lists generally have a very regular structure and are ideal for storage in a database. I won't go into this in detail here because it's covered more fully later in the book.

Stock Levels. Synchronizing your site database with your stock control system allows you to make stock levels available online with no human intervention. I talk more about this in Chapter 16: *Content*.

Customer Product Reviews. You can create a system that allows your customers to post their own product reviews directly on your site, a feature you may have seen in action on Amazon.com. This may seem very dangerous at first (after all, you don't know what they're going to say!) but it can actually be incredibly beneficial. It can increase your credibility dramatically by showing site visitors that you have confidence in your products, and it's a good first step to building a community atmosphere around your company. Good customer reviews are really testimonials, and site visitors will feel more comfortable dealing with a company when they don't feel alone. Imagine being in a huge retail store all alone, not another shopper in sight – you'd begin to question whether you were making a wise choice shopping there. Using an e-commerce website can be a similarly solitary experience, and customer-driven content will help give visitors the feeling that they aren't alone.

It also provides you a great mechanism for obtaining customer feedback!

Suggest-Selling. Suggest-selling is the old "would you like fries with that?" technique, but with a database

> **Astroturfing:** Don't make the mistake of posting bogus "customer" content on your site in an effort to simulate grass-roots support. This practice (referred to as "astroturfing" because it's like fake grass with no real roots) can come back to bite you in the butt – big time. Some major companies such as Microsoft have even hired PR agencies to pose as satisfied customers and post glowing messages in public forums, only to have the practice backfire and cause scathing press coverage and public anger when the practice was discovered. Don't do it!
>
> It's certainly a good idea to have staff active in forums related to your business or industry, but make sure their affiliation is made clear up front.

driven website you can take it to a whole new level of automated intelligence. Once again this is a technique used to great effect by Amazon.com. It can be a difficult concept to understand at first, but from the point of view of visitors to your site it's very simple and powerful – like having an expert standing beside them pointing out other things that may be of interest. The idea is to keep a record of exactly what products all your clients purchase online, then use that information to cross-reference products and predict other things each customer may be interested in.

Let me give you an example. A number of customers go to Amazon.com and buy books by David Siegel about web design. They also buy other books about web design by authors such as Lynda Weinman. Because the site database records all that information, the next time a visitor starts looking at books by David Siegel the website decides the visitor will probably also be interested in Lynda's books. It can then automatically display links to learn more about those other books. Try it for yourself right now: go to www.amazon.com, search "books" for David Siegel, select one of his books such as *Creating Killer Websites*, and have a look down the page. You'll see a list of the other books that purchasers of Killer-Sites found useful.

Customer Preferences. By storing customer profiles in a site database your website can remember visitors and customize itself appropriately according to their preferences and past actions. For example, you can make the purchase process simpler for repeat customers by remembering their delivery details and auto-completing those sections of the order form when they make their next purchase. You can also apply the suggest-selling technique above, and display products that may interest them directly on the home page when they return by analyzing their past purchases and cross-referencing them to purchases by other visitors. This is all part of providing a smooth, personalized website experience to your visitors.

Customer Support. A section on your site for customer support can contain Frequently Asked Questions to reduce the workload on your customer support staff, and detailed knowledge-base articles to assist them with specific issues. Once again, storing this content in a database can make it easily searchable and simple to update.

Data Mining. Once your site has been up for a while and you've been collecting information about visitor preferences and purchases you have a huge potential asset available to you that may not be immediately apparent. Raw data is just raw data, but don't make the mistake of thinking that's the only thing it can be! You can turn raw data into priceless business intelligence by a process known as "data mining". Data mining is basically the technique of examining data to extract useful trends and specific information. The algorithm behind the suggest-selling technique above is a great example: until you perform an analysis of the buying habits of your users, the raw data is useless. But once you process the data to correlate customer interest in different products you suddenly have a very useful insight into customer behavior.

Data also mining forms the basis of the web metrics and web analytics techniques I discussed briefly in Chapter 8: *Objectives*.

I won't go into this in more detail here because it's a huge subject that really deserves a whole book of its own. It's also something that not many developers are geared up to manage yet, but keep a sharp eye on this field in the next couple of years. I guarantee it'll become a hot topic in the near future.

15. E-Commerce Issues
Making the sale

E-commerce (electronic commerce) is not very hard in theory: it's just a matter of using electronic communication tools such as your website to conduct transactions. Sounds simple, doesn't it! E-commerce was just a hot buzzword way back in 1997 but now every commercial site seems to have a shopping cart or an affiliate program. As a result you may think the process of deploying an e-commerce system has become a humdrum, boring affair that anyone can do in their sleep.

It's true that many of the supporting systems such as credit-card processing facilities and shopping carts have now become quite standardized and can be incorporated into a site far more easily than was the case a few years ago, but putting an online sales system in place still isn't a trivial exercise. There are some major considerations you should be aware of if you want your business to trade directly with customers online.

Price structure

Over time most businesses develop a price structure that can become quite complex and cumbersome as new rules and exceptions are added. Rules like "Customer A gets price $X if they buy more than 10 units at a time, but customer B gets price $Y if they buy more than 25 units at a time" become common. Dealing with clients off-line this way may be quite workable if your sales people know all the rules, but translating it into an online version can be a total nightmare for your developer's database programmers.

Try to simplify all your pricing information to a standard structure that allows minimal variations. Every "exception" that must be programmed into the system will increase your development costs.

SSL certificates and secure servers

When you connect to a normal web server with a browser, you send a request for a page to the server which then returns the requested page to you. Both the request and the response are in a plain text format, simple to intercept and view as they travel across the Internet. If you want your customers to enter sensitive information such as their credit card details into your website you need to make sure all the communications between their browser and your web server are encrypted.

This is done using a technology called Secure Sockets Layer, or SSL. By obtaining an SSL certificate (generally referred to as a "cert" in the industry) and having your web server configured to run as a secure server you can protect access to specific pages on your site. If you really want to you can secure your entire site, but SSL connections place additional load on the server and so should only be used for pages that really need it such as the checkout page for your shopping cart.

SSL certs are issued by groups known as Certificate Authorities, or "CA" for short. There are only a few major CAs that are universally recognized, with the market dominated by Thawte (www.thawte.com) and VeriSign (www.verisign.com). VeriSign is a large US company that was the clear market leader in the US but had trouble selling high-grade security products to international clients due to America's ridiculous laws that classify encryption software as a weapon and therefore restrict export. Thawte, immune from US restrictions by basing themselves in South Africa, could sell high grade encryption products to anyone they felt like and pretty much dominated the non-US market. Personally I've used Thawte in the past because I've found them both cheaper and easier to deal with than VeriSign, but then VeriSign bought Thawte in an attempt to dominate the global market so choosing between them is no longer really a choice.

There are other CAs in the market, but not many, and it's an area you need to be particularly careful with. My personal favorite at the moment is InstantSSL/Comodo, a UK-based company that has very fast response times and extremely competitive prices. Check them out at www.instantssl.com.

Hopefully we'll see more competition in this market space and the price of certs (which, quite frankly, is ridiculous – often many hundreds of dollars / year) will start to fall as recent entrants such as InstantSSL undercut the older providers.

Quite apart from security through encryption, SSL certs also perform the job of verifying the identity of the web server to site visitors. Certs are normally issued for a very specific host name such as "www.example.com", and if they are used at a different address (even something at the same domain, such as "site.example.com") the web browser will display a warning to the user and may refuse to enter secure mode at all. This is done for a very specific reason: so that when a visitor goes to a website and enters their credit card details, they know that the site is really who it says it is and not some site put up by J. Random Hacker that just looks like the site for BigCo.com, but actually takes card details and stores them for malicious misuse. When a CA issues a cert they are in effect endorsing the identity of the website that will use it.

That's why obtaining an SSL certificate is not a trivial job. The CA will require that you go through a reasonably rigorous screening process that will involve providing them with documented proof that you actually own the domain for which the cert will be issued, and that you really are who you say you are. In some cases the process can take a couple of weeks, so don't leave your application for a certificate until the day before you launch your shiny new e-commerce site! Some CAs such as InstantSSL can dramatically shorten the process by using automated identity checks, but make sure you factor in time to organize it all in advance anyway. The last thing you want is a site ready to go live and no SSL cert.

End to end security

There are a couple of common sayings in the computer security business. The first is: "The only secure computer is one that is turned off, disconnected from any network and locked in an underground room, and even then you can't be sure." The second is: "I'm paranoid, but am I paranoid enough?"

This attitude goes double when dealing with your customers' financial information and credit card details. A breach of security in your order processing procedure can result in so much bad feeling that it's almost impossible to recover the trust of your customers.

When putting an online transaction system in place you need to think about the overall flow of sensitive information. It's a bit like a chain, one bad link can cause it to break no matter how strong the other links are.

Imagine a simple manual credit card system that might be created by an inexperienced developer: the customer enters their card details into a secure form on your site, and the server then sends the order and card details to you as an email for processing. Hang on, what format is email as it passes across the Internet? Oops, it's in plain text and can be read in transit by a third party without your knowledge. Bzzt, you lose.

Or perhaps the developer is a bit smarter, and decides instead to store the card details on the server for you to access through a secure link once you have been notified of the sale. This could be done by saving the order details in a text file on the web server. But is the site on a dedicated server that only you can log into, or is it just a virtual server with other site owners logging in to manage their own sites and possibly maliciously reading the files on your site?

Oops again, better make sure that text file was encrypted.

A security-conscious developer following good practices will observe a few basic rules:

1. Whenever sensitive information has to move from one location to another, make sure it passes through a secure connection or is encrypted before passing across an open connection.
2. Never store sensitive information unless you absolutely have to: if you can process and delete it immediately, do so.
3. If it must be stored (such as in a file or a database) make sure it's encrypted in case the data store is compromised.

It's certainly possible to handle credit card and other sensitive information in a secure and responsible way, but it takes planning and understanding on the part of your developer.

Accepting credit cards

If you sell your products directly over the Internet, the ideal situation is to have the entire transaction handled automatically up to and including payment processing. If you want people to make credit card purchases from your website there are three basic approaches to making it happen: a real-time payment gateway, manual processing, and phone-back systems.

All three approaches require that you have a "credit card merchant account" with a financial institution such as a bank. This is a special account that allows you to accept card transactions from your clients and have funds transferred from their credit card to you. Obtaining a merchant account can be a painful exercise because the requirements are quite strict: you may have to provide several years of financial records, and / or pay a large security deposit. Feel free to shop around for a merchant account, because it doesn't have to be with your existing bank (although that can help). Most merchant account providers will allow you to stipulate that all incoming funds be automatically forwarded to another account, such as your existing company account at your bank.

The thing to watch with merchant accounts is the fee structure. Most merchant account providers charge a monthly fee plus a basic transaction fee and a percentage of each transaction. These fees are payable no matter how the transaction is handled, it makes no difference whether you are taking credit cards over the counter in a shop or on a website. The actual fees vary on a sliding scale based on transaction volume (both number of transactions and average size) but to give some idea of scale, typical fees for a low-volume merchant might be AU$20/month account fee, plus AU$0.50c per transaction and 4% of each transaction.

A **real-time payment gateway** allows your web server to process credit card transactions totally automatically, and have the funds transferred directly to your bank account. This is definitely the preferred method if you deal with a lot of transactions because it can save you a lot of time on each transaction. However, there are some costs to consider. Firstly there are usually license and setup fees for the payment gateway itself, and these can run to thousands of dollars. Thankfully these fees have started falling and there are good deals to be found now. Secondly there are transaction fees for the payment gateway, typically a base per-transaction fee that may vary from a few cents to a few dollars plus a percentage of the transaction value. Thirdly there are the usual merchant account fees mentioned above – note that your bank (or other merchant provider) is usually separate from your payment gateway, and they both want to make a cut on all your transactions.

> **How do payment gateways work?**
>
> A payment gateway is a system which processes credit cards on your behalf.
>
> Visitors to your site enter their credit card details into a secure form, from where they are securely passed to the payment gateway. The gateway has a direct connection to the banking network and checks the validity of the card and performs a transfer of funds from the credit card to your merchant account. It then returns a result code to your web server to indicate success or failure.
>
> Using this system you never have to worry about storing credit card details on your server: you just pass them to the gateway when required.

A **manual processing** system looks to the customer pretty much the same as a real-time payment gateway: they go to the checkout, put in their credit card details, and the sale is accepted for processing. The difference is that unlike a payment gateway, manual processing just stores the card details to be processed by hand later by your staff. This can be a good interim measure if you already have a credit card merchant account and want to take payments on your website at minimal cost. The customer enters their card details and the server either sends them to you with the order details as an encrypted email, or sends you a simple email notification that an order has been placed so you can log into a secure web interface to retrieve the order details. As far as your order processing procedure is concerned, you can then treat it just the same as you would a telephone order. This approach avoids the payment gateway licensing and setup fees and the gateway transaction fees, but you will still need to pay the normal merchant account fees and your staff time for handling the processing.

Depending on the scale of the project I often recommend to my clients that they start with manual processing and convert to a payment gateway down the track when the transaction volume justifies it.

A **phone-back system** is really just a variation on manual processing, but it can be reassuring for paranoid customers. In this scenario you don't take the credit card details online at all: just the order details plus a contact phone number for the customer. The system sends you a notification message as usual, but you then telephone the customer to ask them for their card details over the phone. This can be very reassuring to the customer because they know firstly that you have received and are processing their order and secondly that their credit card has not passed across the Internet.

It's actually a good idea to allow your customers to elect to use phone-back even if you implement a full payment gateway. There will always be people who would like to make a purchase from your site but don't like the idea of sending their credit card details over the Internet no matter how much reassurance you provide about encryption and security.

Getting Started

Phase 1: Strategic Planning

Phase 2: Design And Engineering

>Phase 3: Production<

Phase 4: Launch / Promotion

Post-Launch: Running The Site

Endmatter

16. Content
It's all about the content

Back in Chapter 14: *Back-End Engineering* I explained how a site can be created in three major components. You'll remember the components are the skin, the content, and the functionality.

Of the three components, site content is the area where you will need to take the most responsibility. In order to allow you to take maximum control of the site content it's very important that your web developer goes to the trouble of separating the 3 major components so that site content contributors don't have to deal with issues of page design, graphics, HTML, and site navigation. All you should have to worry about is the information itself, not how you go about making it look like the rest of the site.

The content creation team

The bigger your website, the more content you will need to manage and the more people you will need to coordinate. Defining roles and a contributor hierarchy will assist with issues of responsibility and approval. There are generally three content-related roles within your organization plus one external role.

Site Editor: Internal staff member with overall responsibility for the site content and has the power to over-rule the decisions of all other contributors.

Section Editor: Internal staff member who oversees a specific section of the site, such as a products section or a reviews section. Material submitted by content contributors generally requires approval by a section editor.

Content Contributor: Internal staff members or subcontractors who supply material for a specific section of the site but do not have right of approval of material. Their submissions may go straight into the CMS (Content Management System – more about these later!) but won't go live on the site until approved by their Section Editor.

Site User: External users who may have minimal content creation privileges, such as posting messages in a public forum or writing reviews of products. Since your website is the public face of your organization on the Internet it's important to make a distinction between areas that random site users can update and areas that are official company material. You may need to place disclaimers to that effect on some pages. Don't set the site up in such a way that posts by site users could be misunderstood to be company policy!

Small sites may have only one or two internal contributors and no hierarchy, and basic content management systems may not provide a content approval system.

Content creation tools

The vast majority of the content you need to supply for your site will be one of three types:

- **Text**, such as company profile material, articles, reviews, etc.
- **Databases**, such as lists of products, lists of dealers etc.
- **Images**, such as product photos.

Other types of content include sound files, video clips, diagrams, animations, and slide shows.

Many web developers require your contributors to either work with software such as Dreamweaver or FrontPage to produce HTML documents directly, or send content in a raw form to their development team who do the final conversion to HTML and then publish it on the site. That means you either have to buy HTML editing software and learn how to use it, or pay your developer every time you want to make an update. Either approach puts a time and cost barrier between you and your website.

If you are creating the actual HTML file for each page you add, the best approach is to have your developer create HTML templates which are write-protected. That way you are always starting with the same standard layout and don't have to worry about issues like placement of navigation graphics. You can then create a new page using the template, and transfer it to the server using FTP (File Transfer Protocol) software once you have added the new content. Once you start going down that path, though, you almost need to become a web developer in your own right - which is probably not why you went into business!

Ideally, content contributors need to be able to work with tools they are already familiar with. For most people that means an integrated office productivity suite such as AppleWorks, Microsoft Office, OpenOffice.org or some other word processor and spreadsheet. If your staff can work with software they are already familiar with you can reduce expenses in terms of additional training and software licenses. The downside of using standard programs is that documents will require conversion prior to publishing on your site. Some word processors provide an "export as HTML" facility, but the quality of code produced is usually so pathetic that this approach should be avoided at all costs. If your contributors will be working in their usual office suite it is far better to have the document conversion handled by a content management system on the server.

Content management systems

The purpose of a Content Management System (CMS) is to sit between your content contributors and the public face of your website, and regulate how the content gets from the contributors to the site. Software-based content management systems grew out of the need to combine traditional publishing requirements such as approval procedures with new requirements specific to web publishing such as HTML document conversion and navigation management.

Back in Chapter 14: *Back End Engineering* I talked about dynamic pages generated using a database back end. Almost all content management systems work on the principles described in that chapter.

Content management systems provide a level of abstraction between the format of the content as prepared and the format as presented on the site, allowing site contributors to provide content in a plain format and not worry about issues like font selection. That way your staff can work in a word processor when preparing a press release, and not have to worry about page layout or the HTML that will eventually be used to present the press release on the site.

The best way to understand what a CMS does is consider a typical sequence of events when adding a press release to your site using a CMS:

1. A writer prepares the text of the press release using their usual word processor.
2. The document is submitted to the CMS, usually via a browser-based interface.
3. Public release and expiry dates are specified for the document.
4. The CMS stores the document in a content database.
5. The editor for the press release section of the site is notified automatically by email that a new item has been added to the CMS.
6. The editor logs into the CMS and reviews the document, making changes as necessary and marking the item as approved for publishing.
7. Any necessary formatting is automatically applied, such as converting paragraph breaks to the equivalent HTML paragraph tags.

8. The standard interface style as used by the rest of the site is automatically applied, including a header, footer and navigation.
9. When the scheduled release date is reached the page is automatically made accessible on the web server.
10. Links from other parts of the site to the new page are created so visitors can find it.
11. When the press release expires, the page is automatically removed from the site and links from other pages are removed.

It sounds complicated, but the beauty of the system is that only a few of those steps require human intervention: the rest of the conversion and scheduling is handled automatically and no HTML needs to be created by the contributor or the editor.

This example includes a scheduled release date, which is a feature that's not generally required for content – you usually want it up there as fast as possible, not at some predetermined time in the future. However, it doesn't include other steps which may be required for different kinds of documents: for example, some documents may need to go through a technical or legal review process prior to publishing approval being granted. High-end content management systems can be told what sequence to use for handling different kinds of documents, or for documents destined for different areas of the site.

Commercial content management systems that provide all these features can be quite complex and expensive, with current market leaders requiring a lot of setup and customization and costing tens of thousands of dollars. If you manage content for a busy newspaper website with hundreds of daily articles and dozens of journalists that price may be a drop in the ocean and you may need every single feature. But for a small business site the cost may be far more than the budget for the entire project, and the CMS may be so complex that no one ever bothers updating the site.

There are other alternatives, however, including some great Free/Open Source solutions like Zope (www.zope.org) and Joomla (www.joomla.org) which are available free on the Internet. These projects aim to provide similar features to expensive high-end commercial CMS packages but without the high cost. This is ideal for mid to large sites but you need to be prepared to learn how to use the content management interface. A fair degree of system administration expertise may also be required to initially install and configure them.

Once it's set up and running a content management systems can a huge time saver even on very small sites. However, many web developers working in the low price range are individuals or very small partnerships with limited technical expertise, and they will probably expect you to learn an HTML editing package and FTP program in order to update the site – or fork out more cash to pay the developer for every little change.

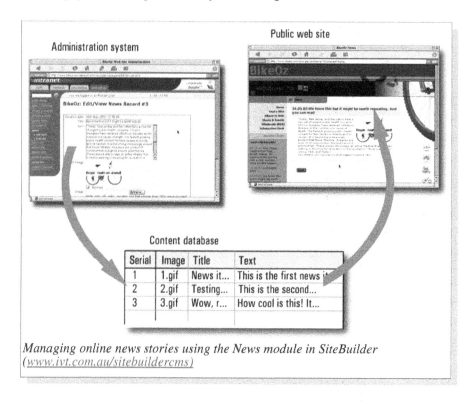

Managing online news stories using the News module in SiteBuilder
(www.ivt.com.au/sitebuildercms)

Some of the latest content management systems do far more than just content management: for example, SiteBuilder (www.sitebuilder.com.au) is an extensive web application framework that in addition to providing regular "content management" features also provides modules for business-specific processes such as handling event registrations; tracking workers compensation cases; managing internal documents including revision control and restricted publishing; inventory management; customer inquiry tracking; stock / inventory management; creation and tracking of gift certificates; managing your contact database; and over a hundred other business processes. High-end systems such as SiteBuilder provide a very high level of integration between the daily operations of your business and your website, allowing your staff to do much of their work directly in a web browser from any computer and giving your customers faster access to information that's specifically relevant to them. As a result your website becomes more tightly integrated into your business and updating it ceases being a chore: updates just occur naturally in the course of daily business operations.

Approval process

When you have more than a couple of people contributing content to your site you can rapidly run into difficulty controlling who can update what.

You may have sections of your site managed by different people: one staff member may be responsible for news items, another for products, another for support resources and yet another for tenders. Sometimes you may even need a team of people looking after a busy section, and that means creating a contributor hierarchy. You may want staff members to be able to add news items to the site, but for them to remain hidden until approved by a News Editor.

Some content may also need to go through more specific review processes prior to publishing such as a legal review or technical review.

High-end content management systems have the flexibility to create different access levels for different staff: some with content submission privileges, some with approval privileges. There may also be special cases where you have multiple contributors with the same access level, but who can't approve their own content – all content needs to be approved by another contributor as a final sanity check before going live. That way at least two sets of eyeballs have checked it without any one contributor having seniority.

Time-critical content

While most web content needs to be published as fast as possible, some may need to be scheduled for release at a specific future date or expired after a certain time. This can include press releases, tender documents, news items, and articles released in installments.

There may be legal ramifications regarding release dates for some material. For example, in some countries all tender information must be released simultaneously in multiple media. Putting tender documents on a website days before the tender is officially opened may breach internal policies or even legal requirements.

Once content has been created for inclusion on your website at a future date there needs to be some mechanism in place to ensure that it's made accessible at that time and not before. With manual publishing methods you may have to actually wait until the scheduled time and upload the file to the web server and create any necessary links to take visitors to it. Advanced content management systems generally provide a facility to handle scheduled publishing automatically, allowing you to set a release date and leave the rest to the CMS. When the scheduled release date comes around the CMS will automatically make the new content accessible on the site and create any relevant links to it.

You may want to have some content on your site expire, too, so it's no longer accessible after a certain date. This may be a general policy such as specifying that all news items should be removed from the site after a certain number of days, or a content-specific requirement such as removing a tender application form after the tender closing date. Once again this can be handled either manually or by your CMS.

Keep in mind that once something has been published on a website it's almost impossible to later remove it from circulation. Once it has been accessed by a user it may remain in proxy caches, browser caches, and search engines for a long time after it has been removed from your site. Some search engines like Google even actively try to cache complete copies of pages in order to allow access to them if the original server goes off-line. And projects like The Internet Archive (www.archive.org) attempt to keep copies of all pages published on the web indefinitely as a historical reference.

So once you've published something on the Internet, you can't take it back.

Data source synchronization

In order to create pages for your site dynamically your web server will need to either run a database containing your site content, or have direct access to one located elsewhere. This means that if your business will be providing product information on your website you will almost certainly need to maintain two databases: the one on the web server, and whatever master database you use in the normal day-to-day operation of your business.

For many small businesses the master database may not really be a database at all, but something as simple as a spreadsheet listing all the available products. The problem comes with changes to your product line: if you only have a few products or make minor changes it may be quite manageable to manually update both databases separately, but changes to a large number of products means double your workload. Much better than updating 5,000 pages by hand, but still not totally painless.

Synchronization with off-line data sources can often be handled in a semi-automatic way. A good developer should provide you with tools to perform bulk imports and exports of products to and from the database on the web server, typically using a common format like comma or tab separated text files. That way you can update the products in your master database offline, export as a text file, import the text file into your web database with a wizard, and the job is done.

In some cases you may want to totally automate the process. For example, one of my clients wanted to display stock level information on their website. We set up a script that automatically performed a dump from their master Unix stock control database several times a day, copied the dump to the web server, and ran an import routine. No human intervention, but stock levels were automatically kept up to date (to within a few hours, anyway). An alternative to this would have been to link the web server live to the master stock control database, but this can introduce security risks so for that particular project we maintained the web server database separately to the master database and settled for automated periodic synchronization.

You can apply exactly the same approach to price updates, share prices, and many other types of content.

17. Writing For The Web
Words are cheap, eyeballs are expensive

Writing for the web is different in a lot of ways to writing for other media. There are a huge variety of writing styles both online and off-line, but there are some general limitations related to the way users read online that need to be kept in mind if your site is to be a success.

Reading rate and comprehension

Many studies have been performed to measure reading rate and comprehension in different media. They universally find that reading from a computer screen is significantly slower than reading from a printed page, while comprehension levels are generally similar. It's accepted that typical readers automatically decrease their reading rate in order to maintain a constant comprehension rate across different media.

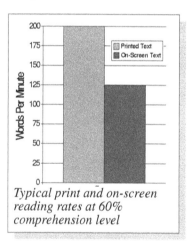

Typical print and on-screen reading rates at 60% comprehension level

The reasons for the decrease in reading rate are mainly related to low screen resolution and a back-lit rather than a reflective reading surface. Most computer screens display text at a resolution of around 72dpi (dots per inch) to 100dpi, while printed text is typically equivalent to 300dpi. This makes printed text appear much sharper to the eye, with around 9 times as much detail per square inch. Computer screens will continue to increase in resolution over the next few years and the development of vector-based interfaces such as used in Apple MacOS X will allow text to become far sharper when displayed on screen at these high resolutions. ViewSonic and IBM have both demonstrated LCD monitors running at 200dpi, giving them more than 4 times the pixel density of other monitors. New screen technologies such as OLED (Organic LED) displays and electronic paper, which works by reflecting ambient light in a similar manner to real paper rather than using back-lighting like current monitors, will also become available over the next couple of years.

The most critical issue as far as copy writing for the web is concerned is that you have less time to get your message across. A typical person reads approximately 200 words per minute from paper at a 60% comprehension level, but reads from a computer screen at only 125 words per minute. This means that given a certain attention span in which to communicate with your readers you have to convey the same message in about half the words.

Reading versus skimming

A major side-effect of a lower reading rate coupled with the generally chaotic, lucky-dip nature of the web is that people generally don't read text on websites in a word-for-word manner. Most people do a quick random visual scan of the page looking for stand-out text elements such as headings, followed by a slightly more in-depth scan of text areas that look interesting. That's true even on pages with large blocks of text such as product information pages. Eye-tracking analysis of a user looking at a web page for the first time shows their attention darting all over the page, picking out the headings and strong visual elements to build a subconscious logical "picture" of the page. The process may only take a fraction of a second and the user won't even be aware they are doing it. They then progressively examine different areas in greater detail before setting on a section of the page to begin reading at a conscious level.

To help visitors through the initial page-scan phase you should block text out in bite sized chunks with appropriate structural and visual cues. Subheadings are your friend when creating text-heavy pages, so use them to show visitors what to expect as they do their initial subliminal scan of the page.

200dpi LCD monitor
Image of ViewSonic monitor courtesy of ExtremeTech

Formality

Because of the decreased word-count available, text on websites should generally be terse. As a result you should make an effort to reduce the formality of your text in order to counter the tendency of terse text to appear impersonal or even rude. Many websites are at least a little humorous but you need to watch localized idioms and customs, and don't use humor at the expense of projecting a professional image. You also need to keep local customs in mind when using informal content: something that may have just the right tone to people from one ethnic group or region may seem totally baffling or even insulting to others.

Pitching the formality of website copy at the right level is probably the second most important thing for a web copy writer to do – after ruthlessly reducing the number of words.

Person And Identity

Once again carefully measured informality is key: if a user is looking at items on your website you want the experience to be more like interacting with a friendly sales assistant than reading an impersonal brochure. The majority of text on your site will probably be third-person but try to fit in some areas where you can justifiably use first-person text as well. Items like customer testimonials and short articles are ideal for this, as are sidebars and bounded items. The objective should be to convey empathy with the reader rather than just talking at them in an impersonal way. Effective promotional copy will build rapport between the reader and your business.

While you may not even be aware of it your business almost certainly has a sense of identity with respect to how it's perceived by customers: perhaps your business is subconsciously seen to be safe, or quirky, or efficient, conservative, trustworthy, progressive, fun, or good value. We all automatically personify businesses that we deal with because as human beings we are wired to understand inter-personal relationships rather than relationships with abstract concepts like businesses. Once our level of interaction with a business goes beyond a certain threshold we start to project human characteristics onto it in order to give our brain some "handles" it can use to define the relationship.

To be consistent in your online branding you should carry your business's identity through to your website copy, although it should be subtle enough that the writing style reinforces the identity without drawing attention to itself. Otherwise your website could be a jarring experience for users: if they are used to dealing with your business off-line and have found you to be very conservative and reliable, going to your site for the first time to find it filled with extremely informal first-person text could totally alter their perception of your business. At the very least it could be a jarring experience, like meeting someone you know well in different circumstances and seeing them behave in a totally different way to what you expect. The natural human reaction is to wonder whether you really knew the person in the first place, and a feeling you can't predict what they'll do next. Businesses should aim to make their relationship with customers as consistent and as predictable as possible to build trust and credibility.

No Spellling Mistaykes

Most business owners would be extremely upset if they ran a big advertising campaign in a prominent magazine only to discover that the ads contained spelling or grammatical errors. The public image of your business is just too important to allow this sort of thing to happen.

Then why do so many companies allow their websites to contain text riddled with errors?

Maybe it's because there is an odd perception that while a brochure or printed advertisement is "real", a website is not. People take far more care when preparing printed material than when preparing text that appears on a website, even though the website may have much greater exposure.

I suspect that a major part of problem is also how easy it is to update websites. A brochure or advertisement is typically prepared by a professional designer who would rather die than send out a final product with spelling or grammatical errors: their reputation would be ruined if they did. Websites, on the other hand, are often updated by some random person within the company without their work even being proof-read or going through an approval process.

Whatever the real reason may be, it never ceases to amaze me how many sites I come across with glaringly obvious spelling mistakes or poorly structured sentences. It really shows that the business owner doesn't care enough about their business to ensure that it projects a professional image. Modern Content Management Systems often include spell-checking facilities, and even if your site can't spell-check it's own content you can still write your copy in a word processor first and then paste it onto your site. At least that way you can spell-check before the text is visible publicly.

Textual errors on your site can dramatically decrease your credibility so you should take as much care in preparing website copy as you would with a printed brochure or advertisement. Hire a professional writer or copy editor if you have to, but most importantly: check *everything*!

18. Multi-Lingual Content
Speak their language

Because the Internet is a truly global medium provision of multi-lingual content on your website may be far more important than for other media. English is the common language of the Internet, and many Westerners overlook the fact that people of all nationalities and ethnic origins use the Internet. In fact, English content comprises far less of the Internet than you may first think. A large amount of technical and scientific content is in German, for example, and the proportion of Asian language content (particularly Japanese) is growing rapidly.

Studies in 1996 showed around 84% of web content was in English, and this number has been falling ever since. Studies in 2000 showed varying results, with between 73 and 80% of web content in English. By 2004 the number was down to around 68%, and it's increasingly common for English-speaking users to find a large number of pages appearing in search results are non-English.

Many browsers already have built-in support for the extended character sets required to display text such as Kanji.

The second most common language is Japanese, third is German, and the rest consists mainly of very small proportions of Chinese, French, Spanish, Russian and Italian. The proportion of English content continues to fall as more Asian companies with a local focus start to use the Internet and infrastructure is improved. My personal prediction is that Chinese will rise to be one of the dominant languages online, rocketing up from 2004 figures of 4% of web content to perhaps 15-20% within just a few short years.

Uptake of the Internet in many non-English speaking countries has been very slow initially, and the most populous countries on Earth (India and China) have been hampered by a variety of factors such as lack of communications infrastructure, economic circumstances, and government policy. Once these barriers start to be overcome the sheer population of these countries will push the Internet further from its English-centric origins.

To meet this growing need Yahoo! has created localized versions in French, Spanish, German, Danish, Norwegian, Swedish, Italian, Chinese, Korean, and Japanese. That may sound like a lot, but Google now has support for 86 languages!

Machine translation

It may be tempting to just run your website through translation software to create a version in another language. However, translation is far more than just replacing words in the original text with equivalent words in the target language. Unfortunately that's about as much as translation software can manage at the moment, and the end result may be understandable but it definitely won't be pretty.

To amuse yourself for a few minutes go to www.google.com/language_tools and type in a couple of sentences. Convert it to another language, then translate the result back again. The more technical the text, the worse the translation will be. How much this matters depends of course on the purpose of the translation.

My advice is don't rely on machine translation. The day is coming when you can feed in a book in English and some software will spit out a Japanese version with impeccable grammar, but it's definitely not here yet. And even when it does arrive, translation is far more than converting language. It's also about converting idioms and finding equivalent but locally appropriate analogies. These things can currently only be done by a human with good knowledge of both languages and, almost as importantly, both cultures.

Navigation buttons and headings

Because site navigation is frequently implemented with images as buttons, you may have to create a whole new set of interface graphics for your site with new text on them. Many icons and symbols cross the language divide quite well, but anywhere that text appears in an image may require a replacement image.

Twice the languages, twice the work

Of course this means your design team will have to create almost an entirely duplicate interface, effectively doubling their implementation workload. And your development team will have to create a system to allow the entire site to be viewed in one language mode or the other. This may require running a CMS that can handle multiple language modes, or it may require the team to create two entirely duplicate sites and place them in different locations. The locations could be different subdirectories of the site with a multilingual entrance page where a user can select their desired language, or they could be totally different URLs (for example with different country extensions, such as www.apple.de and www.apple.hu). This can also help users find your site, since a common trick when searching for local companies is for users to restrict search engines to only display sites within their country.

It's also possible for your web server to make an educated guess as to the preferred language of a visitor based on information gleaned from the browser identification. If you run a very smart CMS with good multilingual support it may allow you to provide the same URL for all languages, and when a page is requested it will decide which is the most appropriate version to send to that user. Very convenient for you, but that can in turn create problems with search engine submissions: when a search engine spiders the site, which language should the server show it? And how do you make the search engine spider scan through multiple language versions?

There are ways around all these problems of course, but providing a website in multiple languages is not a trivial job. There are many potential difficulties, both technical and cultural. In fact, some web developers specialize in doing nothing but creating multi-lingual sites, and have direct access (either internally or on contract) to translators for many languages. If you intend to provide your site in multiple languages you should make that very clear to your developer early in the project because it will influence many of the ways things are done.

19. Hosting
Find your site a home

Web hosting is one of those things that usually happens in the background
without people being aware of it. Many people having a site developed are
surprised when they discover there are ongoing costs involved in addition to
the initial site development fees.

Hosting is a service that is usually given little thought initially, but is extremely
important in the long term. No matter how slick your site is, if you use an
unreliable, low performance hosting service your visitors will get frustrated
and go elsewhere. This is not the place to save a few dollars.

What is hosting?

Once your site has been created it needs to be made accessible to Internet users
around the world. In order for that to happen, it has to be placed on a web
server which is connected to the Internet continuously. If your site isn't placed
on a web server no-one will be able to view it. It's like designing a brochure
and then not having it printed – it's no use to anyone, and it's certainly not
going to help your business.

Hosting companies need to provide:

- The web servers themselves
- Several high speed Internet connections
- Back-up power
- Climate control / air-conditioning
- Physical security of the server room
- Network security monitoring and response
- System administration and updates

Your site sits on one of their servers, waiting for a user on the Internet to type
your website address into their browser. Their browser then connects to the
server and asks for the page, which is then sent back so the user can view it.
Without a web server, none of that can happen.

The first decision to make is whether to host in-house or outsource. In almost
every case the best choice is outsourcing on a virtual server or, if special
functions are required, a colocated or dedicated server at the premises of an
Internet Presence Provider (IPP), also known as a hosting provider. Even the
big boys leave their hosting with the professionals: for example, a colocation

provider looks after the thousands of servers used by the Hotmail service. Running a good hosting system is a very complex job, and a hosting company will be able to do it far better than you could.

Why not host it yourself?

Many businesses have a permanent Internet connection and a member of the IT department anxious to set up (read: "play with") a web server, but running a system for external access by the public has a whole new set of problems associated with it.

Corporate networks are typically run with only one up-stream Internet connection, and generally with just enough bandwidth to fulfill the browsing and email requirements of the staff on the network. Anything more is overkill and wasted money. However, web hosting generates a lot of "bursty" traffic that requires as much bandwidth as you can give it but only for very short times. Actual traffic for a typical site is quite low in volume, with the majority of sites on the net sending less than 10 megabytes of data per day. However, when the site is accessed the data has to be sent as fast as possible or it will seem sluggish to the end user. Big hosting companies have many Gigabits/second of external bandwidth: thousands of times as fast as the Internet connection for a typical company network.

Hosting companies also use a technique called multi-homing, which involves establishing links to several major data carriers and intelligently routing traffic through the most appropriate link depending on its destination and connection load. Multi-homing also improves connection reliability as it frees the hosting company from dependence on any one upstream data carrier. A disaster at one carrier therefore can't take them off-line because they have multiple access points to the Internet.

Virtual servers

Web servers can be expensive items, so instead of using a whole server for every customer, hosting companies commonly use what are called "virtual servers". A single physical server can be configured to handle many websites at once using one virtual server per site. Each virtual server provides a website with its own separate environment, which includes:

- Space on disk to store your website files.
- Remote access to upload new files.
- Traffic logs for your site.

- The scripts used for handling dynamic items like inquiry forms.
- Email facilities for your domain.

The idea is to make hosting economical by splitting the high cost of the server itself across many different sites.

Dedicated servers

A dedicated server is exactly what it sounds like, a real hardware server dedicated to doing nothing but running your website. A dedicated server is when your hosting company provides a whole server for your exclusive use, connected to their network and ready to go. They retain ownership of the server and usually handle things like software security updates and emergency restarts on your behalf.

Obviously this path is more expensive than using a virtual server because the cost of the hardware has to be covered by you alone. However, the use of dedicated servers is rapidly rising for some very good reasons.

Firstly the obvious advantage is performance. If your site is on a virtual server with hundreds or even thousands of others, the server's CPU has to split its time between all the different sites. If one of the other sites on the server gets a massive traffic hit, perhaps as the result of a short-term promotion or event, what happens to your site? It slows down, of course.

The second major advantage is security. With a virtual server the site administrators of all those other sites will be logging on and off all day doing their own updates, and even if they aren't malicious mistakes can still happen. I was doing some work once on a client's site, which at the time was hosted with the client's ISP, and discovered that I was not restricted to the directory of that site as I should have been. In fact, I discovered that I could see everything on the server: the master server configuration, their other customer's websites, all the log files, everything. I immediately phoned the client's ISP and told them of the security problem, which they promised to fix. Two weeks later the problem was still there and my client moved their site to a different provider.

The third major advantage is flexibility. A couple of years ago a website was just a collection of HTML files and images, and you could host it on almost anything. But now with the use of Content Management Systems, shopping carts, and dynamically generated pages, websites are becoming more like a piece of computer software. Software has to run on the kind of computer it was designed for: you can't take a Macintosh program and run it on a Windows computer, or put a Unix program on your Palm Pilot. The same is true of advanced websites. They may need a specific kind of database system, or a certain scripting language. Most virtual servers only provide the basics. To run an advanced website the best thing may be to put it on a dedicated server which is set up specifically to meet your requirements.

Something to keep in mind with dedicated server packages is how backups will be handled. Hosting companies should perform regular backups on all their machines running virtual servers, but you may have to pay extra for backup facilities on a dedicated server.

Server colocation

Another option, which is really just a variation on the dedicated server theme, is colocation. With colocation your hosting provider gives you space in their server room and connections to power and data: you provide the server. Generally you must also take much more responsibility for running the server. If anything goes wrong, you have to fix it. This option is really only for businesses that have server administration expertise but don't want to fork over the cash to build their own hosting infrastructure. Many web developers go down this path because they can colocate one server with a hosting provider and put all their clients on it to split the cost.

Colocation provides the greatest flexibility and control because the hardware and software is entirely your responsibility. With a dedicated server the hosting company provides the server and you may be limited to the options they have available, but with colocation they only provide the space and they don't care what server you run. If you really insist on hosting your site on a custom-modified turbo-charged Commodore 64, colocation is probably the only way to do it.

Extreme performance options

If your site goes beyond the performance requirements of even a dedicated or colocated server there are some extremely high-performance options available to you. I only mention these to give you the big picture because if your site reaches this level of traffic you will almost certainly need your own system administrator with a level of knowledge far beyond what is covered in this book – or at the very least a helpful hosting company willing to build and administer a custom server system for you.

If you're running a database on your site the first step to scale up capacity is to run the database on a separate server: you can have one server dishing out the actual web pages and images and another running the database. This alone can result in a significant performance improvement because each machine can be optimized to do its particular job very efficiently.

The next step up is a "load sharing group", or cluster. A cluster is a number of servers running in parallel with identical content. Traffic is directed to each server in a round-robin fashion. In the event of a problem the cluster should be smart enough to figure out if one of the servers has failed, and stop directing traffic to it until the System Administrator has figured out the cause and fixed or replaced the failed unit. Many high traffic sites run on clusters consisting of a dozen or more web servers in parallel, but from a user's point of view it's like accessing one very high performance server – even if one of the units in the cluster fails.

The ultimate system is a distributed cluster, with multiple servers located in data centers all over the world using intelligent routing to get the data to each user from the closest server. Some of the fastest data distribution networks in the world, like the one run by Akamai for example, work on this principle.

Support

If a system crash brings down your web server at 8pm on Friday, how long will it take to get it back online? Or even realize that something is wrong? Good hosting companies offer 24-hour support and fault response, couple with continuous automatic system monitoring. It's no good if your site is down until Monday morning when the IT staff arrive or if you have to call your hosting company to tell them they've got a problem.

Exactly how much support you can expect from your hosting company can vary widely depending on the kind of package you go for. Perhaps paradoxically, the most basic packages like virtual servers actually come with the best levels of support. Because the hosting company owns and runs the server and has a large number of clients depending on it, they will do everything in their power to keep it running and you can be sure that problems will be noticed very quickly. And because they may have hundreds or even thousands of identical (or at least similar) servers racked up in their data center they will be intimately familiar with them.

With a dedicated server you may theoretically be entitled to the same or greater level of support than a virtual server, but because you are the only one using that particular machine you may be off their radar screen to some extent.

Make sure the hosting company is using an automated monitoring system that will alert them immediately to anything out of the ordinary. They shouldn't be relying on you to tell them when something goes wrong.

With a colocated server you are pretty much on your own unless you specifically enter into some kind of service contract with the hosting company. With a colocation package the provider supplies you power, a data feed and rack space: the rest is up to you. One of the reasons for using a colocated rather than a dedicated server is to allow greater flexibility, so the hosting company may not be geared up for dealing with your particular kind of server and they'll be unlikely to have spare parts on hand. Colocation service contracts often involve basic items like fault-monitoring and email alerts and possibly manual restarts in the event of a total system lockup, but that may be all. Service contract charges usually involve a basic fee that includes status monitoring and a certain number of incidents with additional incidents incurring additional fees. Security patches, software upgrades etc will almost certainly be your responsibility.

Hosting charges

Hosting companies have to cover fixed costs like power, wages and the server itself, as well as variable costs, like the amount of data transferred from your site.

Virtual servers are usually charged on a monthly fee basis, often with a once-off setup fee. Some hosting companies also offer quarterly or annual payment options which can save you money and may be more convenient. The fees charged by different hosting providers vary depending on factors like:

- How much storage space is included (the "disk quota").
- How much data you are allowed to transfer each month (the "traffic quota").
- How many email accounts are included.
- Whether a database can be run on the site.
- Whether SSL (secure server) facilities are supported.
- Optional features like PHP, cgi-bin privileges and FrontPage extensions.

If you exceed the traffic quota they may also charge an additional fee based on a rate per megabyte or gigabyte of data. Beware of hosting plans that advertise as "unlimited traffic", because they're probably lying. No provider could continue to make money while truly allowing anyone to run as much traffic as they like from their servers, so look at the fine print. You'll probably find there is a clause that says they have the right to cut off your site if you use "excessive" bandwidth, but they may not even tell you what they mean by excessive! Better to stick with a reputable hosting company who specifies up front how much data is included with the hosting plan, and makes it clear what you will be charged if you go over that limit.

Providers with apparently similar offerings may vary in price for reasons which may not be obvious up front: things like how much technical support they are prepared to provide, the performance of their network, and how frequently they perform backups.

Dedicated servers are usually priced in a similar way to virtual servers, with a base monthly fee and a fee for traffic over the quota included in the package. Things to look out for with dedicated servers are fees for monitoring and restarts. Because the hosting company supplied and retains ownership of the server they will have to take responsibility for hardware problems. However, there may be a gray area surrounding software and the operating system: with a dedicated server you generally have the right to log in as the root user and do things like install new software and upgrade the operating system, but if you stuff it up, it's your responsibility. You may find the hosting company offers a "managed server" option in which they take responsibility for handling security patches for an additional fee.

Colocation services are also charged on a base fee and an excess traffic fee, but with an added restriction: physical space. The high-tech data centers that hosting companies use are incredibly expensive places to build, and floor space in a data center is some of the most valuable real estate on the planet. That's why they cram lots of sites into each server, and when they provide a dedicated server it will almost certainly be in an ultra-small case designed for use in a data center. It also means that if you want to place an Internet-enabled refrigerator in their data center they'll charge you a wheelbarrow load of money to do it.

Data centers usually use industry-standard rack mounting systems so they can stack computers up on top of each other. Rack mount computer cases are defined in terms of their height which is measured in "rack units", or RU. One rack unit is 1.75" tall. A typical rack has a vertical capacity of around 36 to 42RU, and stands around 6 feet high. The high-density server cases used by hosting companies typically fit an entire high-performance server into a single rack unit case similar in size to a pizza box. Pretty small!

What this means is that if you will be colocating a server with a hosting company they will want you to use as little of their rack space as possible, and they would definitely prefer a server in a standard rack mount case. If you supply a server in a desktop or tower case they will have to use a rack shelf to sit it on, and a lot more vertical space will be used. Colocation plans typically include a limited amount of vertical space, probably 3 or 4RU (5.25 - 7 inches), and if you want to use more you should be prepared to pay extra. If your server takes up a lot of vertical space that's room they can't rent out to another client.

So which should you choose?

When making this decision you should always involve your web developer. In fact, it may almost be a matter of your developer making the decision for you. They will understand the details of the technical requirements of your site and will probably either provide their own hosting service or have a relationship with a provider they frequently work with. This doesn't mean you are tied to their recommendation, but your developer will have a lot of say in this decision.

Here are some rough guidelines to match against your requirements.

Basic site: if you are running a low-key site and don't have any unusual scripting, security or database requirements, go the economical route: a virtual server.

Dynamic site: if you have a site with more than about 1000 products in a database, or you will be taking sensitive data such as credit cards or customer orders that you don't feel comfortable leaving on a shared server, go for a dedicated server. It will be worth it for security and performance.

Specific requirements: if you have unusual database software or absolutely have to use a special scripting language that isn't commonly supported it may be best to go for a colocated server.

High volume: If you have a big database or very high traffic, talk to your developer or hosting company about an extreme performance option such as a server cluster.

Whatever alternative you go for, remember that you aren't committed for life: if you start with a virtual server and discover you need more performance or special features you can always switch to a dedicated server down the track. Switching servers or hosting companies may not be trivial for complex sites but it can certainly be done if required.

Domain name registration

There are some things to keep an eye on in relation to registering your domain name (often done at the same time as setting up hosting).

Firstly you need to be aware of the difference between hosting fees and domain name registration fees, because they are totally separate things and many people get them confused. Hosting fees go to the company that actually runs the server hosting your site, as mentioned above. However, domain names are registered with organizations known as domain registrars, who perform a sort of "directory" service to make your domain name accessible on the Internet. When a user wants to get to your website, the domain registrar directs their browser to your hosting company.

It's actually a bit more complex than that and I don't want to bore you with the details, but all you should need to know is that your domain name needs to be registered so people can get to your site. The end result is that you will need to pay two fees: the hosting fee and the domain name registration fee, and they will probably go to separate suppliers. Even if your hosting company registers your domain name on your behalf you will probably still get a bill from a domain registrar at some point.

This area can be made more confusing by the fact that you may not be billed separately, because there is an increasing degree of crossover between hosting companies and domain registrars. Many domain registrars now provide hosting services on the side, and many hosting companies have reseller deals with domain registrars.

The second thing to be very careful of is to make sure the domain name is registered with you listed as the owner. Domains are normally registered with a number of contact people associated with them, such as an Administrative Contact, a Technical Contact and a Billing Contact. It's quite normal for your hosting company to register your domain on your behalf and list themselves as the Technical Contact because that means they can receive any technical queries and act on your behalf. However, the Administrative Contact is considered the owner of the domain so you need to make sure they list you as the owner.

I've seen some hosting companies register a domain for a client and put themselves down as the domain owner. Then when the client needs to move their site to another hosting company for some reason they find they don't even own their domain – and the old hosting company refuses to release it! This is not only unethical, in many cases it's illegal but that doesn't stop it being a total pain in the butt if it happens to you. Moving a domain, which is a process that should be as simple as an email or logging in with a password to authorize a change, can become a drawn-out legal battle that costs money on both sides and takes your domain offline for days, weeks, months, or forever.

You can check whether your developer or hosting company has registered your domain with you as the owner using a service called "WhoIs", which reports lots of information about domains such as who owns them, which registrar they are registered through and which provider they are delegated to. If you don't have WhoIs client software handy on your computer you can use the web-based WhoIs tool I've put online on the Stay Sane site www.stay-sane.com/whois.

If it turns out you aren't listed as a contact for your domain you should kick up a big fuss right now and tell them you'll go elsewhere unless they get it fixed immediately. Then when it's fixed, move your site to another hosting company anyway. Domain hijackers aren't to be trusted with your business.

Getting Started

Phase 1: Strategic Planning

Phase 2: Design And Engineering

Phase 3: Production

>**Phase 4: Launch / Promotion**<

Post-Launch: Running The Site

Endmatter

20. Promoting Your Site
Spread the word

When companies first consider online marketing they often have the impression that all they have to do is create a site, register it with some search engines, and wait for the hits and the money to roll in. I call this the billboard mentality - expecting that people will be wandering the net, minding their own business and suddenly BAM, they see your site in all its glory.

Sorry to disillusion you, but it doesn't work that way.

First you have to build it, then you have to promote it, then promote it more.

On-demand information

The difference is that unlike billboards the web is an "on demand" medium. There are only a few ways that a web surfer will ever get to your site, and the next three chapters cover each of these methods:

- Knowing the address and typing it in directly.
- Clicking on a link from another website (a reference or a paid advertisement).
- Using a search engine and finding your site in the results.

The problem is that most people put all their faith in search engines to lead people to their site and don't work on other avenues of promotion.

The role search engines play is allowing users looking for a specific product, service or information to seek it out among all the other sites on the net. That might sound like an overly obvious statement, but the critical point to remember is that they have to be actively seeking your type of product or service, or possibly even your specific brand name. People won't get to your site by accident.

Push marketing

One of the most basic principles of marketing is that repeated exposure to a brand builds awareness of it, which is A Very Good Thing. Companies have tried all sorts of things to keep themselves prominent in the minds of their clients and prospects, such as giving away all sorts of useless trinkets with logos printed on them.

Now with the latest generation of database-driven sites there's a new way to get your name out there. One of the most powerful things about the new generation of dynamic websites is the ability to integrate push-marketing functionality, in essence part of a CRM (Customer Relationship Management) strategy. Some systems such as SiteBuilder (www.ivt.com.au/sitebuildercms) have facilities to store your entire contact database and define arbitrary categories. You can then place each contact into one or more categories, and then use those categories to send out email and newsletters just to specific subgroups.

That last paragraph may have left you wondering what on Earth I'm talking about, but a specific example should help.

Imagine you run a hobby shop which stocks a large range of products including model trains, remote control cars, and scale aircraft models. You use your website to promote your product range and also maintain a contact database within the administration system. Then you could define categories of "trains", "RC cars", and "scale aircraft", and place your contacts into one or more categories depending on their specific areas of interest. You can even allow your customers to do this themselves by registering on your website and selecting the categories they are interested in.

Then one day one of your suppliers sends you some promo information for a new scale aircraft model that will be available soon. You want to let your clients know about it, but it would be a bad idea to just email your entire contact database every time something happens because many people couldn't care less. Model train and RC car enthusiasts would probably just see it as an annoying intrusion.

So instead you write up a brief promo message in your CRM, and specify that the message should only go to contacts in the "scale aircraft" category. The system automatically finds all your contacts that are listed in that category and sends the message to them, even personalizing each message with their name so it seems as if you've sent the message just to them. Inside the message is a little blurb talking about the new product and a link that takes them straight to a page on your website all about that product.

And of course because you send news items only to people in a specific category, all your customers receive messages that are genuinely of interest to them as individuals. Your scale aircraft customers never receive notification of a new Flying Dutchman model train, your RC cars customers only get news about RC cars, and everyone is happy. Especially you, since it takes almost no effort and can greatly increase your customers' satisfaction.

Viral marketing

Viral marketing is a technique that few marketers harness successfully, but can potentially have an enormous impact on the success of a product or service.

To learn more about viral marketing, the best place to get started is by reading *Unleashing The Ideavirus* by Seth Godin. Available both as a printed book and online as a PDF, it provides a great introduction to the concepts and techniques of viral marketing. You can obtain both hard and soft copies at Seth's website at www.ideavirus.com.

The short explanation of viral marketing is that it's a marketing message that is spread by people who use your service. The classic example is the Hotmail web-based email provider, which attaches a little promo blurb to the bottom of every message its users send out. As a result all Hotmail users automatically become unwitting marketing agents for the service, exposing their friends and associates to the Hotmail advertising message whenever they send an email.

Other examples include entertaining or intriguing movie files that are released on the Internet with people encouraged to forward it to all their friends. They in turn forward it to all of their friends, and so on.

Viral marketing is potentially one of the most effective forms of exposure you can possibly harness, so I strongly encourage you to check out *Unleashing The Ideavirus* and think about how you can apply it to your business.

21. Multi-Touch Marketing
Leveraging multiple media

"Spiral Branding" is a term sometimes used by Internet marketing consultants, but it's really just a new name for an old-media marketing technique: multi-touch marketing. Both terms are quite accurately descriptive.

The traditional spiral

The basis of multi-touch marketing is that an idea or brand can be reinforced through repeated contact, preferably from multiple sources. The first time someone comes in contact with a brand they almost certainly won't remember it, but by the third time they will. It also allows you to use different media together in a coordinated way, allowing each to do what it does best for maximum return at minimum cost.

With traditional media, multi-touch marketing works like this: a supermarket runs a short TV campaign saying simply, "Watch your letterbox for our new catalog". In a few days the catalog arrives in your letterbox. You've been subconsciously expecting it. The TV ad told you the products in the catalog were on special so you read it and visit the store to investigate, where in-store promos and sales assistants extol the virtues of each product. The store closes the sale.

In a month or two the same "spiral" repeats – TV campaign, followed by letterbox drop, followed by in-store promotions.

Different media, different strengths

You'll notice that in the example above each step of the spiral provides more specific and detailed information than the one before. A 15 second TV spot can do no more than awaken a faint glimmer of awareness, because airtime is far too expensive to use for anything else. Then the catalog provides general info and pricing on the product range at a much lower cost. Finally, once they are in the store, the customer can investigate each product in detail.

While websites aren't much good at doing the initial job of getting someone's attention they can be great in the later part of a spiral because of their ability to provide a great depth of information at relatively low cost. Don't sell your site short and just put up a small quantity of shallow product information and a company profile – make sure there is enough content on it to allow visitors to really get into it and satisfy any questions they may have. Then use your other promotional avenues to direct people to your site for detailed information.

Starting your spiral

To start your spiral, all your non-web advertising – business cards, catalogs, mailouts, yellow pages ads – should include your web address. Your website then becomes your equivalent to the supermarket shop front. It may be a catalog encouraging people to visit your store, or perhaps it's an entire virtual store itself where customers can purchase online.

A website adds a whole new dimension to multi-touch marketing, allowing small and medium businesses to take advantage of a technique previously used mainly by larger companies. Your small, low-cost Yellow Pages ad saying "See our website at..." can be just as effective as a multinational corporation's huge ad saying the same thing.

Landing pages

When you put effort into promoting your website by directing everyone to your home page you're wasting a great opportunity. The home page of a website is usually very general, and visitors then have to find their way to whatever they're interested in.

Rather than list the home page address in advertising, canny web marketers create special "landing pages" for each promotion they run. A landing page is just a page specifically designed to be the next step in a spiral, to draw the customer in and send them off a certain direction within your site or answer specific questions. It needs to be a logical follow-on from whatever advertising you use to direct people to it.

For example, if you decide to have fliers distributed to all the households in your neighborhood with details of a special "buy one pizza, get one free" offer you should create a page specifically about the offer, and put the URL of that page on all the fliers.

To make it easy for people to type you should keep the address as simple as possible, such as "www.example.com/freepizza". Landing pages don't have to be accessible from the rest of your site, either: in fact it's usually better to have a "hidden" page that users can't get to unless they know the address exactly because that way you gain all sorts of interesting statistics about the success of your campaign. Your web server can record every visit to the page, and you can then work out the response rate by dividing the number of visits by the number of fliers distributed. By measuring the response rate of each campaign you can then tune future campaigns based on past results.

Data junkies will no doubt have seen the obvious extension to this: if you create a page for each campaign, why not make it even more fine-grained? Why not create a different landing page for each different magazine you advertise in? One landing page for each target suburb for your flier distribution, and generate stats on response rate by geographic location? Or try distributing fliers on different days of the week, and have one landing page for each day so you can see when you get the best results?

Don't get too carried away though, or you'll end up having to create nonsense URLs just to make them all unique.

If your website runs on a Content Management System it should be relatively easy to add short-term landing pages for special purposes, and the CMS will probably also have integrated statistical reporting so you can see how many people respond. If you don't have a statistics-capable CMS then you can probably extract the same information from your web server traffic reports: see Chapter 25: *Understanding Traffic Statistics* for more information.

Closing the loop: permission push marketing

Once you've established a relationship with a customer or potential customer, no matter how fleeting, your first objective should be to obtain contact details and receive permission to send them email from time to time. Once you have permission to send them email you have a fantastic opportunity to pro-actively keep the relationship alive at very low cost.

What you absolutely should not do under any circumstances is send bulk email to people who haven't asked to receive it: UCE (Unsolicited Commercial Email, otherwise known as spam) is one of the worst aspects of the modern Internet and there have been many attempts to stop it by a variety of technical and legal methods. In Australia, for example, the Spam Act which came into effect on April 10th 2004 requires that all commercial electronic messages including email and SMS must not be sent without the prior consent of the recipient (express or implied), must contain a functional "unsubscribe" facility, and must accurately identify the sender of the message. Most developed nations have similar legislation.

Sending spam can result in a huge backlash against your business. Your mail server could be blacklisted by ISPs around the world, your reputation online can be ruined, and your business may face huge fines. Don't do it! Make sure you comply with the appropriate regulations by including an unsubscribe feature, etc and *never* send commercial email to someone unless you have permission to do so.

Important issues to keep in mind when adding people to your email list are the differences between single versus double opt-in, and passive versus active opt-in.

If you put a newsletter sign-up form on your site where people can enter their email address and be added to your email list, the simplest approach is just to immediately add any email address submitted. That's called single opt-in, since the user only has to do one thing to be added to your list. However, it's an unfortunate fact that there are people who will maliciously sign hapless victims up for dozens of email newsletters without their consent in order to flood their mailbox with unwanted messages. It's much better to set up a double opt-in system, which accepts the user's email address but doesn't activate the subscription immediately. Instead it sends a confirmation email to the provided address and only activates the subscription after they click a "confirm" link in the email. This prevents one person signing up another without their permission, and also verifies that the email address is valid so you don't have to deal with lots of bounced messages.

Passive versus active opt-in is another step to ensure that people really want to receive email from you. When you have users sign up for a newsletter, product registration, tech support or whatever on your site you can include a check box that allows them to consent to receiving email from you. If the box is checked by default, that's considered "passive opt-in". If the box is unchecked and the user has to click it to consent to receiving email, that's called "active opt-in".

Passive opt-in is considered to be a very gray area legally at present. If you have a "please send me marketing email" checkbox already selected in a product registration form, for example, and a customer who completes the form later claims you have been sending them spam, you may not have much of a legal defense. While it sounds like a lot of hoops to jump through the safest approach is to make sure you only collect email addresses using an active double opt-in system, such as having the user manually click a consent box then check address validity by sending a confirmation email before adding the address to your email list. From your point of view it should be absolutely no more work because the whole process of sending and processing confirmation emails can be handled totally automatically by your CRM (Customer Relationship Management system).

If your CRM supports contact segmentation you should also set up a number of categories and allow users to nominate which categories they want to be in. That way you can send information to a targeted subset of your contacts based on their nominated areas of interest.

So how do you tempt users to sign up and receive email from you? There are many techniques, such:

- Offer regular prizes to subscribers
- Allow subscribers to recommend your news updates to their friends and give prizes to people who gain you the most referrals
- Provide high-value content on your site which can only be accessed by subscribers
- Provide timely news and information that people find useful

Don't go crazy with promotions and prizes: while they may attract people initially, the only real way to convince people to subscribe to your email list (and, more importantly, *stay* subscribed) is to send messages that people actually find useful. Keep emails short and relevant, and don't fall into the trap of filling them with sales pitches. If you concentrate instead on sending messages that subscribers in your target demographic will really want to read you'll benefit far more than if you build a massive list of random subscribers who only read your emails in the hope of winning a prize. Prizes are nice, but they're no substitute for high-value messages sent to an email list consisting of people in your target demographic.

For example, I have a subscriber list to which I send messages about website development, site promotion, online security, and new Internet technology. Because website development is my business I know that many subscribers to the list are potential clients: anyone interested in those topics is likely to fall directly within my target customer demographic. By providing them a high-value information service I'm working to build a relationship with them, gain their trust and hopefully convert some of them into customers. If I suddenly started using the list for high-pressure sales pitches I'd lose almost all my subscribers immediately, and I doubt I'd make any sales. If you look at any of the really successful email newsletters you'll see their owners all realize that the trick is to provide real value and to leverage repeated, long-term contact to gain the trust (and eventually the business) of subscribers.

While there are many regulatory and technical hurdles to leap when setting up a permission-based push marketing campaign it's also one of the most rewarding ways to promote your business and build contacts.

22. Site Cross-Linking
Becoming part of the culture

What do you do if your product is not the sort of thing that people generally go looking for? How do you get people onto your travel agent website when they really went online to look for rock climbing gyms in New Zealand?

The biographies mentioned in **Chapter 9**: *Your Target Demographic* are obviously very brief and not representative of all your clients, but creating a hypothetical person will make you think of them as having other interests and desires. This is very important, because it helps you narrow down this particular marketing tactic to a simple exercise: find out where your target demographic spend their time online and then go there to get their attention.

Put yourself in their shoes

So where does your hypothetical person go on the web? Maybe you want to find students about to travel so you can sell them your cut-price adventure tours: they may use online travel agencies looking for the best deal, adventure related sites for background information, and YMCA and Youth Hostel sites for cheap short-term accommodation. Check whether online versions exist for the relevant print magazines, make up a list of all the places your hypothetical person would be likely to go, then do everything possible to get your site exposed there.

Be where your market is

Request a reciprocal link from those sites. Have your service mentioned as a news item on them. Pay for banner advertising if you have to, but only on sites that will reach your target market. Buying 50,000 banner impressions for your adventure tours on a wine review site may not do much good, but that same exposure in the online edition of a snowboarding magazine could help make you an overnight success.

What you want is someone looking for snowboarding information to see your adventure tours mentioned, and think "hey, this looks like fun, let's check it out".

In short, don't limit yourself to for people specifically looking for your service. Grab people sideways who are looking for other related things, and then show them how you can meet their needs.

Case study: Mac Trading Post

Some time ago I wanted a showcase site for an online classified advertisement system so I could demonstrate the idea to a current client who wanted to service a niche market. My company already had a few clients interested in similar things so we knew the effort developing the system would not be wasted.

We settled on creating an online Macintosh second hand guide since it would be the kind of thing we would use ourselves. So once we had the site online we submitted it to 3 search engines (Alta Vista, Yahoo, and Excite) only. We sent press releases to several newspapers, to John Halbig (who ran the Mac EvangeList mailing list at the time) and to a few websites receiving considerable traffic from Mac users. We were mentioned on the EvangeList (200,000 subscribers), featured on Mac News Network, linked from Low End Mac and others, and written up in The Age newspaper's computer section. From day 1 the site took traffic of many thousands of page views per day, with almost no search engine assistance whatsoever.

Result: only about 3 person-days of effort for promotion, and the site almost immediately began sustaining extremely good regular traffic. Most of this came from cross-linking by Mac related sites. We know where our target audience hangs out, so we went out to grab them and drag them in sideways. When they go to Low End Mac they don't intend to go to a Mac classifieds site, but they start thinking "Hey, rather than upgrading I could try selling my Mac, and then buy a newer one". Or they go to Mac News Network for a daily news fix and see the site mentioned and click across to check it out.

Mac Trading Post

Become part of the culture

So my advice is this: become part of the culture, part of the world where your potential customers spend their time. Try to be in their face (nicely!) all the time, get featured in newspapers, get mentioned on sites where your target demographic spend their time. Don't wait for them to search for you.

23. Search Engines
Helping users find you

I've deliberately put this chapter at the end of the section on site promotion because so many people see good search engine rankings as the one and only key to online success, and I wanted to make sure you read the previous chapters first so you could keep everything in perspective.

Search engines are one of those topics where everyone seems to have an opinion: friendly discussions over search engines can rapidly escalate into a religious war. Many people see good search engine rankings as a certain guarantee of success for their website, but that isn't true. Other people think it's too much of a black art and ignore search engines altogether, but that isn't the right answer either. And even those who agree on the importance of search engines often have totally different opinions on how to get the best ranking.

Like the Internet itself, search engines are not a magic answer. They are just another piece of the puzzle.

Search engine basics

A search engine is essentially a big list of websites with a system that allows users to search the list to find pages that match their criteria. When you use a search engine, it doesn't actually look around the Internet right there and then: instead it looks through its huge database of sites that has been built up over time and returns the matches it finds there. You can then follow links to the actual sites.

This has a couple of implications. Firstly, search engines are generally fairly slow at including new or recently updated sites in their database, so search results may be somewhat out of date and may even include pages that no longer exist. Secondly, it would be impractical for them to maintain complete copies of the entire contents of every single website in existence so search results will always be incomplete.

That is not to say that search engines don't produce valid and meaningful results, because they certainly can. You just need to understand how they do their job in order to make the best use of them both as a user and as a site promoter.

Hierarchical lists versus keyword systems

Search engines generally allow two distinct methods of search: browsing hierarchical lists, and searching using keyword systems. Each has its strengths and weaknesses so many search engines now try to combine both.

The classic example of a search engine based on a hierarchical list is Yahoo!, which began as a couple of students publishing their browser bookmarks in a sorted structure so other users could look through them. They defined a number of categories for sites, and when they found a site they thought was interesting they would add it to their list. All sites were added manually. When a user was interested in looking for sites on a specific topic they would browse through the available categories to the area of interest to find what sites were listed there. This means hierarchical lists are very powerful if you are looking for something in a general field but don't know any specific brands or words that you could perform a match on. For example, if a user is looking for a new washing machine but has no idea of what brand they might want they could go into a "white goods" category. However, this also makes it very hard to find matches for specific words if you don't know what category the word may fall into, such as when looking for a company name or scientific term.

The earliest successful example of a search engine using a keyword system was Alta Vista, which began as a technology demonstration and was so popular with Internet users that it became a business in its own right. Search engines like Alta Vista and Google use a system called "spidering", where a program on their server (the "spider" or "crawler") visits websites automatically and examines the contents. It then keeps a record of significant words that it finds. Users can perform searches on those keywords, and it returns a list of all the websites it knows about that contain those keywords. This means keyword-based search engines are very powerful when you are looking for sites which refer to a specific term such as a brand name, but don't know what category they might fall under. It also makes them less useful when searching for a general category of sites when you don't know what keywords might be relevant.

Because the database required to run a search engine is so big and requires so much server hardware (Google has literally hundreds of thousands of servers!) many search engines share the same back-end database and simply use a customized skin to match their own branding.

Some search engines which started out purely as hierarchical lists, like Yahoo!, have added keyword search facilities to appeal to fans of both search methods.

Getting onto hierarchical lists

Because most search engines based on hierarchical lists have real people who manually update the list, getting your site onto them may be a long, slow process. The typical procedure is to go to the search engine and complete a "new site" or "add link" form which generally includes your site name, a description, and what category it should appear in. Your application will then go into a queue to be assessed by a staff member who will approve or reject the listing.

This process can be very laborious, but the result is listings that are reasonably well screened against nonsense entries. It also means that it's very difficult to have your listing updated, because once the search engine staff have gone to the trouble of checking and classifying your site they won't want to do it again unnecessarily.

Getting onto keyword search databases

Keyword databases use an automated system to add new sites. Their spider software automatically follows any links that appear on pages it already knows about, and indexes the contents of those new pages. It then follows links from those pages to find still more, and so on. The process is repeated indefinitely so that the database grows over time as more sites are automatically indexed.

The spider keeps a list of pending pages that it hasn't yet indexed, which includes all the links it finds on pages it has been to so far. But what happens if your site is brand new and no one has created a link to it yet? How will the spider find your site? Easy, your site can be manually added to the list of sites to be indexed. Once again this is done by going to the search engine's "new site'"or "add link" form where you can enter the URL of your site. It then goes into the queue for the spider to index.

Because keyword search systems base their results on a secret algorithm using what they find on the site itself, the form will probably only have an entry for your URL. Other values such as the title, description, and keywords are derived automatically from your site.

Keyword search algorithms

One of the difficulties of submitting to keyword search engines is that the methods they use for site ranking are a moving target. Their job is to allow users looking for specific information to find it, and the objective of site promoters is to have their site appear as high in result rankings as possible as often as possible. Obviously these objectives are directly opposed, and programmers who write the algorithms for search engines keep their methods very secret. Specialist site promoters known as Search Engine Optimization (SEO) consultants are equally ardent about trying to crack the "secret" to good listings in each search engine.

Once again there is no magic answer here, no matter what the latest fad is in the SEO forums. Like most things in life it's just a matter of trying to cover the important things in a logical way.

The most obvious thing about keyword search results is that when a user enters a list of keywords in a search engine it finds all sites it knows about which contain those keywords. But how does the search engine then decide which sites to show first in the results list?

While each has its own variation on the theme, keyword search engine algorithms generally use a secret combination of four broad aspects of a site to determine rankings in result listings: headings and keywords, meta tags, link popularity, and user profiling.

Headings and keywords

Where a word appears on a page can determine how much relative importance the search engine will give to that page. A page that includes a keyword in the title, for example, will have more importance than a page where the word appears only in the body of the page. Other factors such as how many times the word appears on the page, how close to the top it appears, and how close it is to other words in the user's list of search terms may also come into play.

Make sure your site contains plenty of text describing your products and services, since textual content and headings is what search engines pay a lot of attention to when finding search matches.

Note that text which appears in images is invisible to search engines. Humans can read text equally well if it appears on the page itself or in an image or Flash object, but computers have a lot more trouble. Search engines ignore images and other non-text objects, so if your site has all its navigation done with buttons formed by graphics, search engines won't be able to see the text on the buttons. Since site navigation usually consists of words such as product categories it may be extremely important to your ranking in search engines for the labels on those buttons to be indexed. If you have important keywords that only appear on images, make sure they are also included as text elsewhere on the page. Your web developer should also include them in a special section of the image tag called the "alt" (alternate) attribute, which is used in place of the intended image by browsers that don't display images. Websites that use a lot of Flash or have a lot of content in images may have trouble obtaining good search engine rankings.

One special case worth noting is keywords in the URL of your website. Keywords in a URL are generally given much higher importance than keywords located in the content of the site itself. In general, the order of importance is keywords in the URL, followed by the page title, followed by page content, and lastly meta tags if they are factored in at all.

Meta tags

Meta tags are special hidden tags that can be placed in an HTML page for a variety of purposes. Meta tags are not displayed by browsers, but search engines can see them. Meta tags contain information *about* the page they are on.

While there are many different meta tags the most relevant ones in relation to search engine listings are the "keywords" meta tag and the "description" meta tag.

The theory is that if a search engine finds a "keywords" meta tag on a page it can include those keywords in word matches even if they don't appear on the page itself. This means that if you have a page on your site for a specific product, and there are certain words you think people may use when searching for that product but those words don't appear on the page itself, you can place them in the "keywords" meta tag to help users find it.

However, something that even some so-called "experts" don't realise is that almost all search engines have dropped support for the keywords meta tag entirely. By the beginning of 2003 the only major crawler-based search engine to still take much notice of the keywords meta tag was Inktomi. This is because meta tags are obviously very open to abuse by unscrupulous site promoters. A common misuse is to add keywords in meta tags for all sorts of unrelated topics so the page will show up more frequently in search results. As such it's now pretty much a waste of time to carefully and painstakingly craft a keywords meta tag. My advice is to ignore it entirely unless you've got time to spare. Better to concentrate on other factors such as page titles and content.

The "description" meta tag is a bit more useful, but not much. When search engines return search results they include a "page snippet" which is usually the first few words from each page, allowing users to scan down the results and decide for themselves whether they think the page is worth looking at. If a search engine finds a description meta tag it may choose to use it as the page snippet. The description meta tag is therefore your chance to convince users to visit your page in only one or two sentences, and some search engines also factor it into their ranking decisions.

Most search engines nowadays ignore even the description meta tag and create each page-snippet automatically based on search terms.

Link popularity

As should be quite obvious from the previous sections, search engines have learned very quickly that they can't trust site owners to be honest so they now heavily rely on what are called "off-page factors": things they can determine about a page that are not contained in the page itself. The theory is that these factors should be beyond the ability of individual site owners to significantly alter.

The major off-page factor that search engines use is link popularity (sometime called link density).

Link popularity is like a "popularity poll" for web pages. Put simply, link popularity is a measure of how many other websites have links to a certain page. If a page has no other incoming links from other websites its link popularity is 0. If it has 10 websites linking to it, its link popularity is 10. If it has 1000, the popularity is 1000.

The idea goes that if lots of different site owners have created links to a specific page then real people must find that page useful. Search engines therefore assume that other users will find them useful too and so give them a higher rank.

Link popularity doesn't control which sites will come up as a match to specific search criteria, but it can definitely affect how the results are sorted. After the search engine has created a list of sites that match the specified keywords it then calculates the link popularity for each page and factors it in when deciding the order in which to display the results. The actual importance that search engines place on link popularity is a closely guarded secret, but it is generally considered to be one of the most important factors.

Google was the first search engine to build link popularity into its ranking algorithm, which it uses to derive an overall "score" for each page. Google calls that score the "PageRank".

The use of link popularity has been a boon to sites with large affiliate programs because they have a huge number of other sites linking to them. Amazon.com, with one of the first and certainly one of the biggest affiliate programs ever created, has hundreds of thousands of sites linking to it. That automatically gives it a better ranking in search results than a site for a small local bookstore even though they may have exactly the same keywords on them.

This is one of the reasons I always encourage site owners to pursue related sites and exchange links with them: the more sites you can convince to link to yours, the better your search engine results will be.

To check the link popularity of your site (or your competitors!) the simplest way is to use the reporting tool available at www.stay-sane.com/linkreport/. This tool allows you to enter site addresses and generate a graphical report on the relative link popularity of those sites.

An important point to keep in mind is that search engines generally factor in more than just the number of links: they also consider the quality and context of links. One way to do that is for them to go back up the tree a little to also factor in the link density of the sites that link to you.

The best way to understand this is to consider a scenario. All other factors being equal, two websites (we'll call them Site A and Site B) are matched by a search engine as a result of a query by a user. They both have exactly three other sites linking to them. The search engine has to decide whether to display Site A or Site B first in the results, but finds that it can't make a distinction based on keywords, link popularity or any other factor. So it works through each of the sites linking to Site A and Site B, and calculates *their* link popularity. It finds that Site A is linked to by three other sites with very low link popularity, but Site B is linked to by www.amazon.com, www.slashdot.org and www.news.com. Which do you think it will consider more important and put higher in the result ranking? Site B, of course.

This explanation has actually been simplified a lot and a professional SEO (Search Engine Optimization) consultant would tell you I've skipped over a number of issues. For example, link popularity may also be affected by factors such as whether the linking site has its own domain or is only running inside personal webspace (ie: has a '~' in the address), how many outgoing links it has (link dilution), whether the content of the sites is substantially similar, the actual words used to link to your site, and a number of other things.

In short, though, what the use of link popularity in result ranking means to you is that it's not only important to get links from other sites to yours, but particularly to get links from sites that have a high link popularity themselves. By all means go for quantity, but quality matters as well.

One tactic used by some people to increase the link popularity of their site is to register multiple domain names and use each one as a "gateway" to a main site, directing people to the primary content. Then they submit each of these gateway mini-sites to search engines individually, giving the benefit of increasing the link popularity of the primary site.

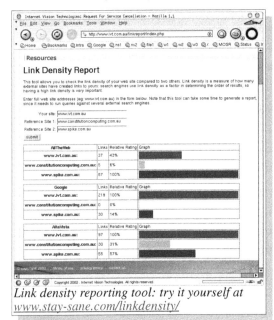

Link density reporting tool: try it yourself at www.stay-sane.com/linkdensity/

By cross-linking the gateway sites, they also increase the link density of all the sites in the mesh which in turn results in a greater factor for link popularity.

Of course it's exactly this sort of result-skewing tactic that off-page factors are meant to eliminate from search results! While this tactic is a hard one for search engines to detect, don't be surprised if they pick up on it pretty fast and penalize your site ranking as a result. If you're going to create a site-mesh try to make each of the mini-sites different and useful in itself – don't do it purely for the sake of search engine rankings. Put some real content on each one, perhaps focusing on a different but related topic for each. Don't just copy and paste the exact same content into each one.

This tactic starts to come up against the effect of diminishing returns: you can spend a lot of effort building a 10-site mesh when you could possibly get better results just by chasing 10 other real sites to link to yours. Building a site mesh may be something to consider doing if you have excess time and promotional budget though (yeah right, isn't that something we all just dream about?).

User profiling

A very interesting recent development is that search engines are now experimenting with user profiling. The basic premise is that not everyone is interested in the same things, so why give everyone the exact same results just because they happen to search for the same terms? Imagine that Bob and Rob both perform a search for "eagles" at the same time. However, Bob likes 70's rock and hates sport, while Rob is into rap and loves sport. What results should the search engine give them?

If the search engine has stored personal interest profiles for Bob and Rob it could factor those profiles into the ranking algorithm, and show Bob a list of Glenn Frey fan pages while showing Rob a list of Philadelphia Eagles NFL Club fan pages. It can take an educated guess about what their search terms mean to them as individuals rather than just showing them results based on a global average.

User profiling obviously has privacy implications even if it's anonymous, but it could ultimately result in search engines finally delivering what they have always promised: search results that are directly relevant to each individual based specifically on their interests and preferences.

Taken to its logical conclusion you could therefore imagine search engines becoming almost transparent intermediaries between users and websites, acting on behalf of each user in a unique way based on their tastes and interests. If search engines become *really* smart there will be almost no point optimizing your site for search engines at all, since they'll cease to have predictable and identifiable ranking patterns themselves. The way they rank your site will be totally different depending on who is doing the search, so the only sensible approach you could take as a site operator is to optimize your site for the type of end user that you want to attract rather than what algorithm the search engines are using this week.

Search Engine Watch and WebProWorld

The single best resource on the Internet for learning about search engines is probably the Search Engine Watch website at www.searchenginewatch.com. This site has been around for years and has built up a great collection of articles that cover all aspects of promoting your site via search engines. Make sure you check it out if you want to know all the nitty-gritty details.

Another great resource and potential black hole for your spare time is WebProWorld at www.webproworld.com, which has very active forums populated by people obsessing over the latest rumored changes in the Google ranking algorithms. There's no better place to track up-to-the-minute tactics and techniques for search engine optimization.

Just be warned that trying to learn about search engines can become an entire career in itself!

24. Customer Service
Working the store

This is it, the moment all your hard work has been leading up to. It's the moment people start typing in your URL and seeing what you've got to say. The moment your site actually starts serving your customers and prospects.

Amazingly, it's also the moment that most businesses fall in a heap.

Imagine what would happen if your company invested considerable time and effort planning, building, stocking and advertising a new store. It's all there, shiny and clean, ready for customers, with all the products neatly displayed in locked cases so people can come in and browse.

Trouble is you forgot to hire any shop assistants!

Visitors come in, see what you've got, and want to make a purchase. They want to take the next step and become a customer. The store is open – but there's nobody home. They wander around, get frustrated, and go to the store down the road.

That's exactly what it's like when you create a website and think your job finishes the moment the site goes live. Better stick around, because it's just the beginning.

Customer inquiries

Customers on your site have very similar needs to people in a real store, including the need to ask questions. Of course part of the point of a website is to shortcut this process by providing immediate access to a lot of information, but you can't predict everything in advance. The purpose of your site is to act as part of a larger conversation between you and your customers. You need to make sure a mechanism is put in place to allow that to happen.

To make the process as painless as possible for your customers you should formulate a policy for inquiry follow-ups, which will include:

- Who will perform the follow-up
- A method for recording the inquiry
- An acceptable response time

When someone is looking at your website and has a question you have a very short window of opportunity in which to satisfy them. If you can do it within a few minutes (ideally so they receive a response before logging off their current Internet session), great. If it takes from a few hours to a day, most people will be fine with that. If it takes days to get a response from you, it will make you look very bad to the customer.

The most common downfall I see with sites run by small businesses is just not checking their email. It's like taking out a Yellow Pages ad and then not answering the phone when it rings. If you have a site, and people are going to try to make contact with you, your published email address should go to an account that is checked at least a couple of times each day – preferably even on weekends

Instead of having all email inquiries go directly to a specific staff member's address such as sally@example.com, have it go instead to a generic address such as info@example.com. You can have mail to that address automatically forwarded to Sally's account, and that way you are covered if Sally takes a day off or leaves the company. Just forward the public address to a different staff member rather than have all the inquiries pile up unanswered in Sally's mailbox.

Designate specific staff members to handle email inquiries, and put a big sign over their desks that says "Answer all email same day" or "Answer all email within 1 hour", or whatever you decide is an acceptable period for your business circumstances. Set an acceptable response time that is as short as you can practically manage.

Anything longer than 24 hours is just plain rude.

Live online service

Newer technologies and techniques are giving site owners more ways to increase the level of personal service available online. Examples include IM (instant messaging) systems, real time text chat, and live voice chat. If you have a permanent Internet connection such as cable, DSL or a T1/E1 and the staffing infrastructure to support it, one or more of these could help you provide a level of customer service that will inspire your site visitors to tell all their friends.

IM software allows users to type messages and have them displayed immediately on another user's computer. The most popular IM systems at the moment include AIM, Google Chat, and Jabber. By publishing an IM account address on your site you could have customers chat live with your sales or support staff.

Web based real time chat is similar, but instead of requiring custom software to be installed by each user it just takes place inside a web browser directly on your site. It's a little more limited than IM because it does not provide warning that a user is wanting to chat and doesn't allow simple direct file transfers, but has less of a barrier to people who may not want to install IM software and register an account just to talk to your customer service staff.

Voice chat requires users to have speakers and a microphone on their computer, and basically turns it into a sort of telephone that doesn't make calls via the normal telephone system – they pass across the Internet. After downloading software or a browser plug-in, users can click a button on your website to initiate a voice connection. The call travels across the Internet to your system, where it goes from a special computer into the telephone system and is directed to your inquiries line or call center. Your staff can receive it just like a normal phone call, but the user hasn't even had to leave your website.

The feedback loop

Over time you need to actively monitor the questions and feedback you are getting from users contacting you via your site, and use it to tune your approach. You may find that a lot of customers have similar questions, which may indicate that you need to provide more information on your website about that particular topic (or make the answers more obvious if they're already there!). The information you gather about your customers' actual experience with your site will be invaluable when you get to the issues raised in Chapter 26: Maintenance And Updates. Use it to improve processes and the experience of dealing with your company for future and repeat customers.

Holistic customer service

The most important thing to remember is that your website is not a set-and-forget tool, it's part of your overall customer service methodology.

Good online resources for learning about issues related to customer service include the HBS Business Knowledge website at hbswk.hbs.edu/, an initiative of Harvard Business School that contains a wealth of information on business matters, and the Customer Service section of Articles911 at www.articles911.com/Customer_Service.

25. Understanding Traffic Statistics
Lies, damned lies and web statistics

Most people find numbers very boring. However, you may be surprised to find that examining your site statistics is a lot more interesting than you expect. Perhaps it's the voyeurism of watching what people do, I don't know, but many site owners find it fascinating. Traffic stats are also extremely important to the ongoing success of your site, since they are the metric by which you can measure the popularity of different sections and adjust your approach accordingly.

Page counters must die!

Many people think that in order to find out how many people have visited their site they need to put a visible counter on their home page. Wrong! As you are about to learn you can obtain much more useful information by generating a traffic report from your server logs instead. A visible page counter just makes you seem amateurish, gives away information that you probably don't want other people to know and probably clashes with the visual design of your site. Don't use one!

Hits must die!

To discuss traffic stats we first need to agree on a standard unit of measure. Unfortunately, most people use the term "hits".

They have this vague idea in the back of their mind that a hit equates to how many people visit their site, but they're not quite sure how or why. They just know that big numbers are good, and huge numbers are even better.

I cringe every time I hear people use a big-sounding hit count to brag about how popular their site is because it's a dead giveaway that they don't really understand how web pages work. In most cases the term "hit" is almost meaningless, and hit statistics can easily be fudged to artificially inflate the numbers.

So what is a hit really?

When a user's browser loads a web page it first contacts the server and asks it for the HTML page itself, and then once it has received the page it requests each object (such as a graphic) included on the page. Every request to the server counts as a hit, whether it's a request for an HTML page or a graphic that appears on a page or some other object such as a movie file.

That means for a typical corporate web page which may have several header graphics, plus navigation buttons, a page background, and some product images, there may be a large number of hits recorded for just one page to be viewed by one person.

The more objects there are on the page, the more hits that will be counted for that one page view. If there are 24 objects on the page, and you count the HTML page itself as one hit, that's 25 hits for one person to view one page!

So someone boasting they've had 25,000 hits to their server may have had only 1000 visitors. In fact, if the visitors looked at an average of 10 pages each there were probably only 100 visitors in total.

Now don't get me wrong, 100 visitors may be very good for that site, but it's very important that you know what you are really measuring. Don't be impressed by someone spouting meaningless figures like "We had 25,000 hits to our website last month". Those 25,000 hits certainly don't mean they had 25,000 visitors.

So if hits are bogus as a unit of measure, what should we use?

Page views

A far more meaningful measure is "page views", which as the name suggests is simply how many times a page has been viewed irrespective of how many hits each view required.

Or to put it another way, one page view is just one person looking at one page. If you have 100 people look at 10 pages each, that's 1000 page views. It doesn't matter if each page had 2 graphics on it or 100, the pageview number is exactly the

---

Faking It: To show how useless "hits" are as a measure, here's a trivial way to artificially inflate the figures for your site. Of course I don't recommend really doing this!

Create a tiny graphic (maybe 1 pixel square) the same color as the background of your page. Duplicate it so you have 90 copies. Then add all 90 images to the bottom of each page. Because they're the same color as the page no-one will be able to see them, but they're each counted as a hit by the web server when the page is loaded.

Assuming your site already had 9 real graphics on each page (say a logo plus 8 navigation buttons) every time a visitor accesses a page it will now count as 1 HTML page + 9 real graphics + 90 dummy graphics = 100 hits. If just 200 people visit your site, and they look at 5 pages each, you can tell all your mates at the pub that your site had 100,000 hits! The numbers are totally meaningless of course, but it sounds impressive.

Hit figures are dumb. Don't use them.

same.

Simple.

Site log files

So where do site statistics come from? Where is all this information recorded?

Every time a web server receives a request for a file ("hit") from a browser, it records the details in a log file. These details will include at least the date and time of the request, the name of the object that was requested, and the network address of the visitor's computer. It may also include other information such as:

- How long it took to send the object.
- The size of the object.
- The type of browser software used by the site visitor.
- The operating system of the visitor's computer.
- The "referrer" (what link they clicked on or page they loaded to get there).
- The "type" of the object (image, HTML file, etc).

This log file can then be periodically parsed (or processed) by a program that generates a report.

Accessing traffic statistics

All good hosting companies provide you with some form of online report generated from their server logs. If yours doesn't, move your site elsewhere. A site traffic report is such as fundamental part of a web hosting package that only really crummy providers don't generate them.

The reports generated by hosting companies are generally adequate for most situations, but if you really want to perform your own analysis on the raw data it may be possible for the hosting company to provide you with the raw log file itself. You can then run a statistics program on your computer to process the log and generate extremely detailed reports, often down to the level of tracking individual users through the site. You won't be able to identify who the users are, but it can still be educational to see how they go through the different sections of your site and compare that to your original plan. Be warned, though, log files can be huge: for very high traffic sites they can be gigabytes in size.

Among the most popular traffic analysis programs are Analog

(www.analog.cx), Webalizer (www.mrunix.net/webalizer) and AWStats (www.awstats.org). These programs can read through large logfiles and generate site traffic reports with customizable levels of detail.

While the headings may vary, most site traffic reports contain sections similar to those listed below. It would probably be helpful to have the traffic report for your site open in front of you when going through the rest of this chapter.

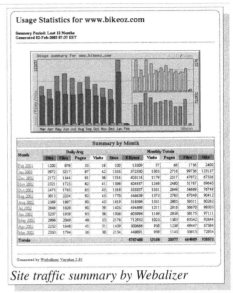

Site traffic summary by Webalizer

Traffic summary

Most reports start with a general summary that notes the total number of hits for the period analysed, the total volume of data transferred from the server, how many distinct hosts (users) accessed the site, etc. There won't be much detail in this section, but it shows some useful overall numbers.

Request ranking

This is probably the most useful report, because it shows which files are most accessed. Look at the first file listed - that is the single most accessed file on your site. It may be a page, or it may be an image that is referenced from many pages.

If it's just a slash ("/") character, that is what's known as the "root" of the site, which is the home page: this is what the server records when a user puts your web address in their browser without any file name: eg, **www.example.com**.

Working down through the list will show you what your visitors are least and most interested in, perhaps giving you an indication of where to focus your efforts in the future. Or it may show that certain parts of the site may be a little hard to find, and the site navigation may need tweaking to bring traffic into those areas.

Pay most attention to the files that end in "html", "php" or whatever extension is used on your server to signify an HTML file. Those are the "pages" that are being viewed. All the files ending in "gif", "jpeg" etc are images that are used on those pages. By looking down the list to see all the pages you can get a good idea what parts of your site people are visiting most often.

Some traffic reports provide a separate report for page ranking, which is really just a request ranking report with all the image files removed to make it easier to compare pages.

Top 30 of 514 Total URLs					
#	Hits		KBytes		URL
1	1734	1.41%	22207	3.88%	/flash/bikeozmovie.swf
2	1638	1.33%	8753	1.59%	/bikeoz.css
3	1229	1.00%	19786	3.46%	/
4	608	0.49%	10469	1.83%	/search.php/search_type/rcta/
5	582	0.47%	15902	2.78%	/search.php/search_type/rcta/search.php
6	321	0.26%	4191	0.73%	/gallery.php
7	318	0.26%	5162	0.90%	/search.php/search_type/bia/
8	301	0.24%	6133	1.07%	/resources.php
9	256	0.21%	3277	0.57%	/where_to_ride.php
10	228	0.19%	12294	2.15%	/search.php/command/search/search_type/rcta/
11	217	0.18%	5342	0.93%	/search.php/search_type/bia/search.php
12	205	0.17%	3167	0.55%	/aboutrcta.php
13	154	0.13%	2162	0.38%	/main.php
14	152	0.12%	1795	0.31%	/shows.php
15	147	0.12%	14	0.00%	/rcta.php
16	136	0.11%	13	0.00%	/administration/users_list.php

Request ranking report

Visits

A visit is a bit of a nebulous term, but it basically means a period when a specific visitor is looking at pages on your site from the time they arrive to the time they leave. So if a visitor arrives at your home page, goes through a few sub pages, then follows a link off to somewhere else, that's considered one visit.

The problem is that your web server itself can't really know when a visit starts and ends. It only deals with individual requests, and doesn't know what requests in particular form a "visit". This is where the traffic analysis software will start making some educated guesses. For example, it might assume that the first time it sees a computer at a certain network address make a request it will consider a new "visit" to have started, and all requests from that address from then on will be considered part of the same visit. Then if a break of more than 30 minutes occurs, it will consider that visit to have ended.

As you can see it's a relatively imprecise measure, but a visit report can still give you a good overall feel for how many distinct people have visited your site and how many pages they looked at each while they were there.

Entry and exit pages

If your stats package tries to make guesses about visits it will probably also make guesses about entry and exit pages. An entry page is the first page viewed on a visit, and the exit page is the last page viewed before the visitor went somewhere else or quit their browser. These reports are also only best-guesses, but once again they can be very informative if you treat them as indicative of trends rather than precise figures.

One thing you'll find is that while many people come to your site through the home page, a lot don't. They may come from search engines that link to pages deep within your site, or from bookmarks of internal pages. Pay attention to the most popular entry pages because it is the content on these pages that is primarily bringing people to your site.

Time report

Many reports include a trend graph of hits or page views over time, allowing you to compare the traffic level from week to week or month to month to see how your site promotion is going. This is a good report to pay attention to in the long term, as it will show trends: whether your overall site traffic is growing or not.

You may also have time reports by day of the week and hour of the day, which will show you when people are looking at the site. Not so useful, but interesting nonetheless: you can see whether people are visiting your site during their lunch break at work, or logging on in the evening after getting home. But keep in mind that the time report will be based on the timezone of the server itself, and visitors may come from different timezones!

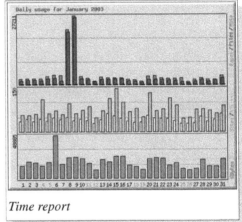

Time report

Domain report

Depending on whether your server is converting the network addresses of users to host names or not, you may have a report which shows which domains are accessing your site.

This report is a breakdown of the "Top Level Domains" (TLDs) that your site visitors come from, and will help you determine where in the world your visitors are located. Are there lots of ".edu" domains listed? Then you probably have lots of visitors who are students or teachers. Is ".br" the highest domain on the list? Then you know that Brazilians love your site. Keep in mind that the domain of many visitors cannot be determined, and some domains may be misleading - for example ".com" domains are often American, but not always. TLDs like .com may be located anywhere in the world. Still, this report gives a good idea of the general overall trend for your site.

Most extensions will be fairly obvious because they are usually derived from country names, but if your report doesn't include explanatory labels you can translate them using the list of TLDs that you can find online at www.stay-sane.com/domains.

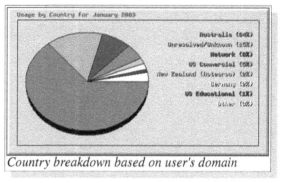

Country breakdown based on user's domain

Browser report

While they aren't very interesting to most people, browser report figures are important to site developers. They show what browsers and types of computers are accessing your site, which allows better planning for future development work. For example, if you see that the vast majority of your visitors use recent browser versions you could perhaps put more emphasis on technologies like Macromedia Flash.

My company doesn't generally include a browser report with site traffic reports because they are only useful on specific occasions. They can easily be generated when required, such as when planning a site redesign. They are not something you should generally care much about unless you're doing site development or redesign.

Referrer report

The referrer report is extremely important when it comes to marketing your site. Whenever a web browser follows a link that leads to a page on your site (for example, following a link inside your site, or a link to your site from a supplier's site, a link from a personal homepage, etc) the server records where the visitor came from. The top lines in this report will inevitably be your own site of course, because each time a visitor clicks a link from one page to another inside your site it is counted as a "referrer", but the interesting stuff comes a bit further down. Look for listings of personal home pages, your business associates, search engines, industry sites, etc: that's where your visitors are coming from.

Many referrer reports hide referrals from within your site and only show those that come from outside, because those are the ones that matter.

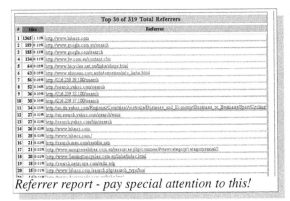

Referrer report - pay special attention to this!

By investigating how visitors find their way to your site you can better formulate methods to promote it in the future. You may find a certain business's site is sending a lot of traffic your way, indicating that you should approach other similar businesses and ask them to link to your site as well. Or you may have had a lot of success with a certain search engine but find that other search engines aren't sending anyone to your site, in which case you should adjust your site and resubmit to the other search engines to try to achieve similar success there.

Working through this section of the traffic report and acting on what you find is one of the most important ways to increase your site traffic over time.

26. Maintenance And Updates
It's not carved in stone

One of the most powerful things about a website is that it isn't carved in stone and intended to remain unchanged for a thousand years. One of the biggest mistakes you can make when taking your business online is to invest time, money and effort into creating a site and then sit back and ignore it. Think of your site as a living creature, growing and adapting as people use it and content is updated.

From time to time you will need to perform maintenance in three very distinct areas:

- Site content
- Site functionality
- Site skin (or interface)

Each type of maintenance has very different requirements, corresponding directly to the three structural layers described in Chapter 14: *Back-End Engineering*.

Content updates

When it's first set up your site will start with well defined functionality, within which there will be the meat of the site: the content. For example, typical functionality might include an online catalog. The content for that functionality will be the details of the products within the catalog. The functionality itself may not change very often but the content may change very frequently. Prices may change, new products may be released, and old ones may be taken off the market. It's vital that you keep the content up to date, otherwise the functionality will become useless over time. The most common form of website stagnation is starting with up-to-the-minute content, then falling farther and further behind and alienating users who become frustrated with not getting the information they want.

Management of content is one area that really sets good web developers apart from Dodgy Brothers Inc. If your developer "hard codes" all the pages of your site and expects you to edit the HTML yourself or pay them extra cash to make changes every time there is a trivial product update it may reduce your initial site development costs marginally, but it will increase your maintenance costs immensely. A major change, such as applying a price drop across your entire product line, may be almost as difficult as creating your site again from scratch. On the other hand, if your content is separated from your site and held in a database which can be easily updated without editing the site itself you can reduce your maintenance costs significantly. And because updates can be performed very quickly your site will have more immediacy and relevance than sites which are rarely updated.

This is especially important with content that has a very repetitive structure and frequent changes, such as product information. An inexperienced web developer may create 1000 different pages for a site with 1000 products, while a good developer will create one page "template" and a database that contains the details of all the different products. The same template can then be used to display every single product simply by specifying to the database which product the visitor wishes to see. To the site visitor this is totally transparent and the site may work in exactly the same way as one with hard-coded product pages, but the difference from a maintenance point of view is enormous.

My preferred approach is to place as much content as possible in a database on the server, and create a special password-protected system that allows the site owner to log in and perform updates. This is known as a "Content Management System", or CMS, and it allows site owners to make changes to the content of their sites using just a web browser, at any time of day or night, and have the changes instantly reflected on the site.

A typical CMS is broken into different sections to match the areas of functionality of the site, such as sections for News, Products, Orders, etc. While the site owner cannot usually change the overall structure or design of the site using the CMS, they can keep the content up to date very easily.

In cases where the website displays information which is identical to an off-line database such as a stock control system, my company sometimes also sets up a system to periodically perform bulk updates on a predetermined schedule. For example, we may set the server to update its stock levels every 24 hours by connecting to an off-line database and re-synchronizing the data, thus allowing site visitors to see recent stock levels. While this will lead to higher initial development costs, automatic database updates can save you effort and therefore expense down the track.

The next step beyond this is to link your public site in real-time to other back-end systems such as a stock control system using "web services" implemented using protocols like SOAP (Simple Object Access Protocol) or XML-RPC. That's a whole extra level of complexity, though. If you go down this track make sure your developer really knows their stuff when it comes to network and application security.

Functional updates

After examining your site traffic reports and listening to user feedback you may decide that visitors are interested in seeing more features on the site. For example, an online car dealership may wish to add a loan calculator and an accessory showroom.

Adding functionality to a site should be done carefully because the navigational structure is generally tied to functionality. Changes to the navigation of a site should be made with great care, otherwise you can end up with a "spaghetti site" with links to obscure sections and visitors lost in a maze. Make sure that new functionality fits into the overall plan of the site, and keep a map of the site so you can see how visitors may travel through it. This is really a matter of revisiting the procedure outlined in Chapter 11: *Site Structure And Focus*.

Keep in mind that if you make changes to the navigation of the site you will probably have to update every single page on the site to reflect the changes. This is where the problems of hard coded pages really stand out - with 1000 hard coded pages, you have to change 1000 files. With a template linked to a database of 1000 items, you only have to change the template.

It's still not an exercise to be undertaken lightly, though, and navigational changes should be subjected to a rigorous analysis process. You particularly don't want to alienate regular users of your site who may be disoriented by changes to the navigation they have grown accustomed to.

When modifying a site to add new features it's usual to also update the Content Management System to reflect the new feature. For example, in the case of the hypothetical car dealership with a new loan calculator there could be a section added to the CMS to allow the site owner to update the default interest rates displayed.

After adding a new section to your site you should generally go through the process of re-submitting your site to search engines as outlined in Chapter 23: *Search Engines*. New functionality generally means new keywords and possibly a wider potential audience.

Cosmetic updates

Visual styles change over time and your company colors and logo may be updated from time to time. Your site should always reflect your current corporate image. A site with current content and functionality may still occasionally require a visual redesign or update to keep it in line with your other marketing materials.

Like other updates, the process of updating the "skin" of a site is really a matter of revisiting previous steps: in this case Chapter 12: *The Design Brief* and Chapter 13: *Design Concepts And Drafts*. However, you should now have the benefit of user experience to guide you when making design decisions. User feedback may tell you that certain pages are hard to read due to a choice of fonts, or that your navigation buttons are indistinct against the background due to a choice of colors.

If you are planning a cosmetic update and haven't received any user feedback, ask for it: place a feedback form on the site, or arrange for some friends to go over the site and make suggestions as a kind of informal usability study.

Larger web developers can often arrange more formal usability studies if required, using testers from your target demographic and compiling the results for you. This may be more accurate than doing tests yourself with friends, as your friends may not want to make negative comments about your site. It's also more structured and objective, since a formal usability study will generally involve setting users specific tasks such as finding a product that matches a certain description and then timing the period taken to complete it. These figures can then be used as a reference point when testing new designs.

Your developer should have kept the skin of the site as separate as possible from the content and functionality. This is another area where database-driven websites are streets ahead of sites with thousands of hard-coded pages. Changing the skin of a site should be a fairly painless process if the site was created the right way in the first place, using interface templates to determine final page layout. This doesn't mean it should be done frequently, though: you need to strike a balance between keeping the site fresh and up to date, and alienating visitors who may feel lost if the site looks different every time they visit. Coming back to your site should be a comfortable, reassuring experience for regular visitors.

Maintenance budget

Although it can vary dramatically depending on your site a good rule of thumb is to allow at least 30% of the development budget of your site annually for maintenance. Discussions with your developer regarding the long-term strategy for your site can help clarify your budgetary requirements, and spending some time to plan the site structure to make updates simpler may save you money in the long run.

Content updates will almost certainly be required, and if your site has been planned well you should be able to perform most of these internally. But even if your site has been created with a CMS and you can keep the content totally up to date without spending another cent with your web developer you must still allow sufficient time to do the updates. You may decide to delegate a junior staff member to spend 2 hours each week keeping prices up to date. Work out what you pay them per hour, multiple by 2 hours times 52 weeks, and add a bit more to allow for unexpected major updates. You may be surprised that even a small commitment such as this can add up to thousands of dollars per year, but you need to be realistic about it. You may intend to perform all the updates yourself and therefore not pay wages to anyone, but do the calculation anyway. Your time is valuable, and you have to allow for it. Otherwise you may find you don't have the time to do updates anymore and haven't allowed the budget to pay someone else to do it for you.

Functional updates will generally require the biggest expenditure, since it will involve your web developer making changes to the site that will probably affect the site navigation and overall site structure. Because adding functionality to a site is usually the biggest post-launch expense I often plan for it well in advance by breaking the development down into a series of stages right at the start of the strategic planning phase. If you have the intention of adding specific functionality some time after the site launches, make sure you communicate this to your web developer as early as possible. Allowances can then be made for future functions.

The cost of functional changes can vary dramatically so talk it over with your developer and budget accordingly.

Cosmetic updates can vary from changing some buttons to giving the site an entirely different look, but if you are intending to perform a major overhaul you should probably allow about 25-40% of the cost of the original site development. Obviously this may vary greatly, but from a developers point of view I usually find that my time and costs for developing a site are divided into about one third design, one third content processing, and one third functionality.

27. The Journey Goes Ever On
That's not all, folks!

So, what now? Where to from here?

This is not the end: as I hope you now understand, a functioning website is not an end result. It's a starting point.

Don't just close this book, quit your browser and forget about it all. This book is really just a way to whet your appetite. There are lots more things to learn and to try.

What follows is a list of resources that are well worth getting your hands on. I hope you'll take the time to follow through on them because they'll open your eyes to a whole range of new possibilities far beyond what I have included in this book. This guide is essentially a relatively straightforward walk-through of the process of site development, while the books listed here will give you a better idea of both the technical specifics and the spirit of doing business on the Internet.

The Cluetrain Manifesto, by Rick Levine, Christopher Locke, Doc Searls, and David Weinberger.

www.cluetrain.com

This book is a couple of years old now, but the ideas in it still don't seem to have really sunk in for most people. *The Cluetrain Manifesto* will open your mind about how business can use the Internet. As the book attempts to illustrate, business isn't about rules and strategies and procedures: it's fundamentally about people communicating. Markets aren't just built and controlled, rather they self-form around that communication, and anyone who wants to be successful in business on the Internet needs to understand how the process takes place.

Unleashing The Ideavirus, by Seth Godin.

www.ideavirus.com

Available both as a hard copy and as a free PDF download, this is a book that practices what it preaches: that some ideas are like a virus, replicating through society at an amazing rate. If you wish your marketing was like that, read this book. It will show you how to turn your marketing into something that will take on a life of its own, spreading in a way you couldn't have imagined. And yes, by listing this book here I'm effectively a carrier of the virus, but this is one I'm very happy to pass on.

Don't Make Me Think, by Steve Krug
www.sensible.com
The subtitle says it all: "A Common Sense Approach to Web Usability". This book should be compulsory reading for anyone who has a say in how your site is designed, either graphically or structurally. If visitors find your site hard to use, they just won't use it – it's as simple as that. This book shows you how to make your site as easy to use as possible.

The E-Myth Revisited, by Michael E. Gerber
www.e-myth.com
Despite its name this book has nothing directly to do with e-commerce, or in fact electronic-anything: in this case the 'E' stands for "Entrepeneurial". Subtitled "Why Most Small Businesses Don't Work And What To Do About It", this book should be required reading for anyone taking their business online. It aims to change the mindset of business owners and managers by helping them systematize their business.

Drilling Down: Turning Customer Data into Profits with a Spreadsheet, by Jim Novo
www.jimnovo.com
Measurability is one of the greatest things about running an online business. It's possible to obtain hard figures on just about every aspect of user behavior on your site. However, sometimes it's hard to know what to do with all those figures. Data is no good unless you can interpret it, and that's what *Drilling Down* is all about.

Planning Your Internet Marketing Strategy, by Dr. Ralph F. Wilson
www.wilsonweb.com
If your business is going to be successful online you need to have a purpose: it's not enough to just create a site for the heck of it. This book walks you through the critical planning stages of developing a purpose and a strategy for your online business, ensuring you aren't wasting time with things that aren't

likely to work. I can't recommend Dr. Wilson's writings enough: he's an Internet veteran who writes classic after classic. Make sure you check out his other publications too.

Secrets Of Successful Websites, by David Siegel
www.secretsites.com/classic
David Siegel was in many ways responsible for triggering the paradigm shift from "Web as text medium" to "Web as graphical medium" with his seminal work *Creating Killer Websites*. His follow-up book, *Secrets Of Successful Websites*, examines issues relating to the management of website development projects. Although it's primarily aimed at developers rather than business owners and is now quite old (there are classic quotes like "more than 300,000 businesses in the United States now have access to the Internet" – I think more people in my *suburb* have net access than that now!), you may still find it a fascinating and useful insight into how larger web developers manage their projects.

Getting Started

Phase 1: Strategic Planning

Phase 2: Design And Engineering

Phase 3: Production

Phase 4: Launch / Promotion

Post-Launch: Running The Site

>Endmatter<

Appendix A: How Does This Web Thing Work?

Even if you've been using the Internet for a long time it would be a good idea to skim this chapter. While you may have a good understanding of how to use the Internet, I'll explain a few things specifically related to web development that you may not have fully understood before.

What are the Internet and the web?

Right from the outset we need to get something clear: the web is not the Internet, and the Internet is not the web. Many people use these terms interchangeably, but they are quite different. The Internet, for all the hype that surrounds it, is merely a way to connect a lot of electronic devices such as computers together so they can share information. The Internet itself is the wire, optic fiber, routers, network hubs and switches, modems, and all the other things that go into connecting those computers together so they can talk to each other. While it provides a method of moving information, the Internet really doesn't care what that information is. It could be a piece of email, a web page, or even a voice conversation or video stream: as far as the Internet is concerned, it's all just data to go from one place to another.

The Internet is used for all kinds of things other than the web. We are now seeing many services previously running on dedicated networks moving to the Internet. One good example is the telephone: phone calls have traditionally been carried on a dedicated telephone network, but many phone companies now use the Internet to carry voice traffic. You pick up the phone to talk to your Aunt in San Francisco, and your voice travels through your telephone to the local exchange, then onto the Internet and across it to the SF exchange, then down to your Aunt's phone. And the thing is you probably didn't even realize the phone company used the Internet to handle the call.

With this sort of ongoing convergence the Internet will eventually be a sort of "mega-network" that connects everything together, from video telephones to domestic appliances.

The World Wide Web is just one particular use for the Internet. It's based on a series of "protocols" (rules that define how information is moved between computers) and "browser standards" (which control how that information is displayed to us humans).

Protocols

Web pages are sent from a web server to your browser using a protocol called "HyperText Transport Protocol" (abbreviated HTTP – when you see a web address like "http://www.ivt.com.au," that's what the "http" part stands for). The standards governing the underlying protocols of the Internet are reasonably static. For the most part HTTP is a good, stable protocol that can do the basics required of it, so there is little reason to modify it. There are also a number of other protocols, such as HTTPS which is the "secure" version of HTTP.

Local caching

Technically, when you view a web page you are downloading it. But the download is not permanent, and it's handled automatically by your browser without even telling you what it's up to. This means you can open a web page in your browser, walk to the wall and pull the modem cable out of the phone socket, and the page won't instantly vanish from your browser window. The browser can keep displaying it because the page has already been sent to your computer. Viewing a web page is not like using a telescope to look at a picture held up by someone a long way away, it's more like having that person make a copy of the picture and send it to you so you can look at it close up. You don't intend to keep the picture forever, but a quick copy is sent to you to look at temporarily and then throw away.

When you move from one page to another your computer may still keep a copy of old pages in memory or on your hard disk. This is called caching, and is done so that if you change your mind and hit the "back" button it can display the previous page again almost instantly without having to go all the way back to the server and ask for another copy. After a certain period of time (which could be when you quit the browser, or when the page gets too old, or when too many pages have been cached) your browser will delete the local copy from the cache.

Browser standards

Once the file has arrived back at your browser it's examined and compared to predefined rules(browser standards) to determine how to display it. Your computer then displays the page on the screen for you to read. Unlike the underlying transport protocols like HTTP and HTTPS, browser standards are fluid and constantly changing. The basic language that all browsers should understand is called HTML, or HyperText Markup Language. HTML allows web designers to define such things as where a new paragraph should begin, what color to use for text and where images should be located on the page. The HTML standard is defined by an organization called the World Wide Web Consortium, or W3C (www.w3c.org). The W3C publishes the HTML standards publicly for anyone to read, and anyone can get involved in the decision making process to determine what changes should be made for the next revision.

Theoretically all browser programmers should write browsers that work to the standards defined by the W3C. I say theoretically, because browser companies have been remarkably bad at doing so. Early competition between Netscape Communications and Microsoft resulted in both browsers deviating from the W3C standards in an effort to outdo each other with more or better features. Unfortunately this had a nasty side effect: as each browser became bloated with additional, non-standards compliant features they became more unreliable at correctly handling basic valid HTML.

And as the W3C revises the HTML standard, the browser companies revise their browsers to add any new features defined by the W3C. The end result of all these revisions is dozens of different browsers, each with many release versions all behaving slightly differently with the same web page. Add to this mix the variations between computer types (for example Macintoshes, designed for accurate color reproduction in pre-press use, generally have a "lighter" display than Windows PCs which are designed to use a darker display to make colors more vibrant on screen), and creating a website that looks good in multiple browsers on multiple computers becomes even harder. The situation has become so bad in recent years that many web developers have banded together to form the Web Standards Project (www.webstandards.org) to lobby browser makers to achieve standards compliance and to encourage users to switch to browsers like Mozilla which attempt to faithfully follow standards.

Without at least some degree of compliance to the HTML standards it's very hard for web developers to control how pages look to the end user.

HTML

When the web was originally conceived way back in 1989 the intention was that pages would be all text with no images. Pages were to be designed on the basis of the logical structure of the content, and HTML did not include any way to control the placement of text or images on the page. It was intended that how a page was displayed would be left entirely up to the browser software. For example, a line of text could be defined as being a "level 3 header". One browser might decide that all "level 3 header" text should be displayed as 14 point Times bold, while another might display it as 16 point Arial. The important thing was the logic and content of the page, not where things were placed and what they looked like. There was no way to specify that a header should be placed 16 pixels in from the left margin and spaced 4 pixels above the body text, for example, or that an image should be located at a specific place on the page.

In fact, the whole concept of a "page" is different to what you may be accustomed: web "pages" have no physical dimensions or proportions, since they can be any size that the user's browser or screen size specifies and can scroll vertically or horizontally indefinitely. That is the main reason why designing for the web is so disconcerting for designers from a print media background: placing objects in an absolute position can be very difficult, and in many cases undesirable. Over the years many tricks and techniques have been developed to allow greater control over object placement and page structure and HTML has now been supplemented by CSS (Cascading Style Sheets) to give greater stylistic control. Web developers generally try to design pages that automatically re-size themselves to accommodate different display sizes, by allowing text areas to expand and re-wrap to suit whatever width is available.

The whole area of the philosophy and method of designing for varying screen sizes is so big that many books have been written on the subject. This is an area your developer will have mastered already, so suffice it to say that laying out a page has many difficulties and limitations and some things which you think should be easy may turn out to be quite hard. It may also lead to compromises in terms of which browsers will be supported, because designs which can be displayed in some browsers may not always work in others or may be displayed in a mangled way.

The domain name system

When you type a URL (Uniform Resource Locater, or address) into a browser, the first thing your computer does is convert the URL you have given it into a numerical IP address. The IP address defines the exact network location of the server from which it must retrieve the file. It then sends a request to that IP address containing a few bits of information, including what file it wants to retrieve, what type of browser it is, and your network address so the server knows where to send the response. The request travels across the Internet to the server, where it's examined to determine what action is required. The server then looks for the requested file, packages it up and sends it back to the address given by the request.

Appendix B: Initial Project Questions

These are questions you should ask yourself before you start having a site put together. There are lots of questions here, and the list can look pretty scary when you see it all together like this.

Actually, I want it to scare you because it can be tempting to jump into creating or redesigning a website without thinking it through. Your developer will need access to a ton of background information to do their job properly, and this list of questions will give you some idea of the things they will need to know. They may ask you some of these questions directly and work the others out for themselves. By the time your site is finished they should be able to recite the answers to all these questions in their sleep.

And so should you.

1. Why do you want a website?
2. What do you want your website to do? (generate leads, online sales, provide tech support, etc)
3. When do you want it to start achieving these things?
4. Are you currently using the Internet? For what?
5. Do you have a registered domain name?
6. What business are you in?
7. What business do your customers think you are in?
8. What business do your staff think you are in?
9. What are your core products or services?
10. What are the 3 main benefits your customers receive from using your products or services?
11. What are the main areas of interest in your target market?
12. How has that changed and how will it change in the next 3 years?
13. Who do you want to reach (consumers, technicians, middle managers, students, etc)
14. How big is your target market?
15. What percentage of your target market use the Internet already?
16. Which geographic regions or areas do you currently operate in?
17. Into which regions would you like to expand?
18. What product information do you provide new customers, old customers and staff?
19. What are the main areas of expertise in your organization?
20. What are the top 5 questions your customers ask before they buy from you?
21. What are the top 5 questions your customers ask after they buy from you?

22. What questions are frequently raised about your business, industry, products and services?
23. What information could you give away free that would be valuable to your customers?
24. How will online marketing change your industry in the future?
25. What research have you conducted on your customers needs, wants and preferences?
26. Who are your current competitors?
27. What are they currently doing on the Internet?
28. What are they doing well?
29. What are they doing badly?
30. What other things could they be doing on the Internet?
31. How would you judge the success of your website? What will you use as benchmarks?
32. What types of businesses are complimentary to yours?
33. What 3 types of businesses would make the best strategic alliances on the Internet?
34. What off-line strategic alliances do you already have in place?
35. What are these businesses doing on the Internet?
36. How can you make your site compelling and habit forming for visitors?
37. How can you use different media for your site? (sound, animations, video, VR, etc)
38. Will you use your site to develop an email database of visitors?
39. What do you have that you could regularly send people via email? (NB: not company news, it'll bore people - product or industry news is much better)
40. What useful and valuable interactive tools could be built into the website? (quote calculator, materials quantity calculator, etc)
41. Does your site have to make sales for you in order to be judged "successful"?
42. Would you like your customers to be able to use credit cards for online transactions?
43. Will customers fax an order form in to you?
44. Can you sell COD?
45. Do your customers want to access account status information online?
46. Will parts of your site need to be updated automatically? (stock levels, etc)
47. How much site management do you want to handle internally? How much to outsource?
48. Are you using email/web within your business yet?
49. Which email/web software are you using?
50. Have you allocated budget for both site development and ongoing

maintenance?

51. Over what time period do you want to see a return on investment?
52. How much time will the online business take to manage? Who will manage it?
53. What training will your staff need?
54. Will you want to create some of your own online content?
55. Do you have a formal marketing strategy?
56. Do you have a formal corporate image definition?
57. What traditional media do you use?
58. How can you incorporate details of your site into your other sales information?
59. How will you let people inside your company know about your site?
60. How will you let your existing clients know about your site?
61. How will you let potential clients know about your site?
62. Does your receptionist understand how to give web and email addresses?
63. How will you follow up inquiries you receive?
64. Who will be responsible for performing that follow up?
65. How can your staff and clients be involved in continuously improving your site?
66. How will you receive and collate user feedback about your site?
67. What do you need today to plan ahead for 2, 5, 10 years time?

Appendix C: Developer Selection Matrix

Some criteria allow a score range: for example, under "General: Quality of their own site" you could rate each company anywhere from 0 to 10. Some involve a multiple of a score: for example, under "General: For each site similar in design or functionality to the one you want built" you would give a score of 30 if they had 3 such sites. Some involve an absolute score: for example, under "Project Management: will assign a producer to your project who does not do any technical work" you would score 40 for any such developer. You can find a spreadsheet version of this selection matrix at www.stay-sane.com/developermatrix.

Web Developer Selection Matrix					
Criteria	Range	Developer 1	Developer 2	Developer 3	Developer 4
General					
Quality of their own site	0-10				
Quality of portfolio sites that relate to yours	0-20				
For each site similar in design or functionality to the one you want built	10				
For each site they have created for a business in your industry	10				
Referrals from people you trust	0-30				
Project Management					
Will assign a producer to your project who does not do any technical work	40				
Demonstration of a clear development methodology	0-40				
Quality of their extranet and ability to track project progress	0-40				
Past clients commend their project management skills	0-50				
Design Strength					
Overall design skills	0-40				
They can write Javascript, Shockwave animations, Flash, rollovers etc	0-30				
Demonstrate ability to design sites with different "looks"	0-40				
Designers are accomplished in other media	0-30				
Technical Strength					
Overall technical strength	0-40				
Can complete or subcontract specialty work such as photography, sound	0-20				
Ability to design websites with both legacy and future browsers in mind	0-30				
Can write Perl, PHP or other server-side scripts in-house	0-30				
Ability to develop databases in-house	0-30				
Marketing Strength					
Ability to write a promotion plan for your site	0-20				
Can assist with obtaining cross-links from related sites	0-20				
Can perform search engine submissions	0-10				
Can perform marketing and design in other media	0-10				
Cultural Fit					
Their overall enthusiasm for your project	0-30				
Personal chemistry, overall feeling of wanting to work with them	0-50				
Ability and energy to help solve your business problem	0-40				
	Score:				

Appendix D: User Profile Worksheet

Name: _____

Age: _____

Sex: [ ] M   [ ] F

Internet expertise: [ ] Beginner   [ ] Intermediate [ ] Expert

Employment status: [ ] Full time   [ ] Part time   [ ] Retired
[ ] Unemployed [ ] Student

Income: _____

Marital Status: [ ] Single   [ ] Married

Computer Type: [ ] Windows [ ] Mac   [ ] Linux   [ ] Other

Computer age: [ ] 0->1 years [ ] 2 years [ ] 3 years [ ] 4+ years

Internet Connection: [ ] Modem   [ ] Broadband (DSL/Cable)

Time online / week: _____ hours

Hobbies:

_____

_____

Notes:

_____

_____

_____

_____

Appendix E: Design Brief Worksheet

These questions have been designed to help you define what you want your website to look like. If you can provide more information than is requested here, great!

1. Existing website

Do you have an existing site? If so, what is the URL and are there any particular design elements that you want to retain or specifically want to change?

2. Corporate Image Specification

Do you have an existing corporate image specification? If so, please provide details (use an attachment if necessary).

3. Corporate Colours

What are your corporate colours (if any)? Note that this needs to be more specific than "blue and grey" – which blue and which grey? Provide some form of objective colour definition, such as a Pantone number, RGB or CMYK code. If necessary, provide actual samples.

4. Logo

Provide a copy of your logo in electronic format as a vector file or a high resolution image, preferably separated from the background layer so it can be used on different backgrounds.

5. Other Marketing Material

Provide copies of existing marketing material, such as brochures, posters, product data sheets etc.

6. Stock Images

Provide any additional design resources, such as product images or stock images that may have been used to create existing marketing material.

7. Website Examples

List 3 to 5 websites that you like, and explain what you like about the design of each one. Even better, take the time to complete a complete Site Critique form for your favorite sites.

Site URL 1: _____

Comments:

_____

_____

_____

Site URL 2: _____

Comments:

_____

_____

_____

Site URL 3: _____

Comments:

_____

_____

_____

Site URL 4: _____

Comments:

_____

_____

_____

8. Target Demographic

Provide a profile of typical website visitors. Better still, complete a couple of copies of *Appendix D: User Profile Worksheet.*

9. Site Structure

Outline the major sections of your website and details of any section that may need its own specific layout (for example, a chat room will probably require a very different layout to the rest of your site).

10. Banners And Ads

Are any banners or other advertising going to be displayed on your site? If so, what are the dimensions in pixels and the preferred location on the page?

11. Baseline Technical Requirements

Are you prepared to prevent some visitors from accessing your site in order to make use of technologies such as Flash? Do you want to cater to as many Internet users as possible, or is there a reasonable cut-off point for the browser version that will be supported? Keep in mind the expected technical expertise of your typical visitors.

Appendix F: Site Review Form

Use this form to help you perform an assessment of your competitors' sites, or of your own site prior to (and then again after!) a redevelopment. It acts as a checklist-based assessment mechanism that will give you an actual numeric score at the end. Make a few copies and use them when browsing the web.

To use the form, spend some time looking over the site with this checklist in hand then go through each specific question and circle "Yes" or "No" as appropriate. If in doubt about any point, answer "No". Once you finish you can add up all the Yes answers to give the site a score within each subsection and a Total Site Score at the end.

For your convenience I have also created an online version of this form which even adds up all the results for you automatically and provides a report for you to print out. It also allows finer-grained assessment of each criteria rather than just a "Yes/No" response, and uses a better scoring system. Check it out at www.stay-sane.com/sitereview.

Reviewer Information

Reviewer Name: _____

Reviewer Email: _____

Review Date: _____

Connection: [Modem] [ISDN] [Broadband]

Browser / Version: _____

Screen Resolution: _____

Site Information

Site Title: _____

Site URL: http:// _____

1: First Impressions

1.1	Does the site make you feel welcome?	Yes	No
1.2	Does it make you want to stay?	Yes	No
1.3	Does it make you want to return or bookmark the site?	Yes	No

1.4	Does it give a clear idea what you can do on the site?	Yes	No
1.5	Can you easily see who owns and runs it?	Yes	No
	Subtotal 1:		--

2: Communication / Content

2.1	Does the site convey a clear sense of its intended audience?	Yes	No
2.2	Does the site convey a clear sense of its intended purpose?	Yes	No
2.3	Is the content appropriate to the purpose of the site?	Yes	No
2.4	Does it use language in a way that is familiar and comfortable to you?	Yes	No
2.5	Is it conversational in its tone?	Yes	No
	Subtotal 2:		--

3: Accessibility

3.1	Is load time appropriate to content, even on a slow modem connection?	Yes	No
3.2	Could you view the site without downloading any plug-ins?	Yes	No
3.3	Is it functional with your screen resolution/browser?	Yes	No
3.4	Are add-on technologies (Java, Javascript, ActiveX, Flash etc) or other "enhancements" (animated GIFs, etc) used only when appropriate?	Yes	No
3.5	Are links large enough to be usable by visitors with limited hand mobility or eyesight?	Yes	No
	Subtotal 3:		--

4: Design

4.1	Does the site use repeating visual themes to create a consistent, clearly recognizable "look-and-feel"?	Yes	No
4.2	Is page length appropriate to site content?	Yes	No
4.3	Is the site appropriate in its use of color?	Yes	No
4.4	Does it avoid juxtaposing text and animations?	Yes	No

4.5	Does it provide feedback whenever possible?	Yes	No
	Subtotal 4:		--

5: Navigation

5.1	Does the site use (approximately) standard link colors?	Yes	No
5.2	Are the links obvious in their intent and destination?	Yes	No
5.3	Is there a convenient, obvious way to move among related pages, and between different sections?	Yes	No
5.4	Is it easy to get to a specific piece of information?	Yes	No
5.5	Does the site provide a search facility and/or a site map?	Yes	No
	Subtotal 5:		--

6: Maintenance

6.1	Does the content appear to be maintained and up to date?	Yes	No
6.2	Is the site free of dead links?	Yes	No
6.3	Is the site free of broken scripts?	Yes	No
6.4	Is the site free of non-functional forms?	Yes	No
6.5	Is the site free of broken images?	Yes	No
	Subtotal 6:		--

7: Credibility

7.1	Is the site free of spelling or grammatical errors?	Yes	No
7.2	Is there a simple way to contact the site owner?	Yes	No
7.3	Does the site have a clearly stated Privacy Policy?	Yes	No
7.4	Does it only link to sites that you would consider reputable?	Yes	No
7.5	Would you trust statements made on the site?	Yes	No
	Subtotal 7:		--
	Total Site Score (out of 35):		--

Appendix G: Copyright Online

Did you know that if you've hired a web developer to create a site for you, your developer may actually own the rights to your site even if you've fully paid for it?

Do you know what content you can put on your site without being in breach of copyright, or what you can do if someone copies part of your site without your permission?

These are serious issues, and if you are responsible for running a website you should have at least a passing understanding of copyright as it applies to websites. Please note that while the information I provide here is in accordance with the guidelines of the Australian Copyright Council (www.copyright.org.au) you should not take it to be legal advice. If you need legal advice, contact a lawyer specializing in copyright law.

Copyright basics

There are many myths about copyright on the Internet. Some people even think that once something has been published on a website it becomes public domain, and they can copy and use it without a second thought.

Wrong. Dead wrong.

Copyright law applies the same way to content published online as to content published in other media such as a hard-copy book.

In short, copyright is a mechanism to protect the rights of people who create certain kinds of material. That material could be written (such as an article), or it could be a design (such as a logo), or it could be software (such as a computer program). Note that things covered by copyright are tangible items: things which cannot be covered by copyright are intangible and include ideas, concepts, techniques, and information. That means, for example, that if you have a great business idea which you write down and show to someone else, copyright will not stop them using the idea without your permission but it can stop them using the specific words you used to describe the idea in writing.

Contrary to popular belief there is no requirement to specially mark material with a symbol or copyright statement for it to be covered. Copyright is automatic, and applies from the moment the material is created. If something has been written down it is probably covered by copyright law, no matter what context you see it in. If an article is published on the Internet, anyone who copies it for their own use without the permission of the author is in breach of copyright.

Copyright jurisdiction

Copyright law has very minor local variations, but almost every country in the world follows the guidelines of the Berne Convention so for everyday purposes you can consider that copyright is the same everywhere and without respect for international borders. Someone in Sydney who copies and re-uses an article originally published in Germany is as liable for breach of copyright as someone in Berlin who does the same thing.

Being geographically remote is no protection against charges relating to breach of copyright.

Copyright ownership

Except in certain specific circumstances the copyright owner is the individual who created the material. That means if you hire a freelance designer to create a design for your website, you do not own copyright on that design even if you have paid to have it created. The copyright rests with the individual who performed the act of creation.

The same applies to other material that may be created on your behalf, such as a freelance writer you hire to provide articles for your site.

Assigning copyright

There are two common ways that copyright for material like a design or article can be assigned to an owner other than the original creator: if the copyright is assigned in a contract, or if the material is created as "work for hire".

Assigning copyright by contract is quite straightforward: the two parties enter into an agreement that the copyright will be assigned by the creator to the new owner, perhaps in exchange for a fee, and it's done.

The concept of work for hire is that copyright on material created by an employee of a business is automatically assigned to the business if it was created in the course of their employment. So if you have a staff member create a site design as part of their job, your company owns the copyright. If you hire a contractor to create the same design and you do not enter into a contract assigning the copyright to you, the copyright stays with the contractor.

If you hire another business such as a web development company to create your site for you, the parts of your site created by the development company probably belong to the company itself if it was created by employees of that company.

Copyright on sites

Copyright law applies to websites in three very important ways: to the design or "look" of the site, to the actual content on the site, and to any software used to manage the site.

As mentioned previously, copyright on things like the design and content of your site may rest with your developer or consultants unless you have a contract with them that states otherwise. Those two areas aren't too hard to get your head around, since most people are familiar with the concept of something like a design or a piece of writing being a created work.

Where things can become a little trickier is with respect to software used by your site.

This is becoming a much bigger issue as more sites become dynamic: a site isn't just content anymore. As this book has shown they can often be more like a piece of software, and many sites use commercial, custom written or open source software running on the server in order to make them work. Note that I'm not talking about the operating system of the server: all servers need an operating system to run, but no-one would consider it constitutes part of the site any more than you'd consider it part of a document you create with a word processor. What I'm referring to is software commonly called "middleware", things like scripts that create dynamic pages on your site and without which the site would not be able to operate without redevelopment.

So who owns that software?

In most cases ownership of computer software is just like ownership of written material: whoever actually wrote it owns it, unless they did it as an employee or assigned the rights to someone else.

Think of it this way: if you purchase Microsoft Office, and use it to create documents as part of your business activities, do you own the copyright on Office itself? Of course not, the copyright is owned by Microsoft. By paying a fee you become a licensee of the software and can use it for certain purposes, but you don't own the copyright to the software itself, only documents that you create with it.

In the same way a Content Management System used to run a large website may be used to create new pages on the site. However, the site owner almost certainly won't own the copyright on the CMS itself unless they wrote it personally. The CMS is a software package, like Office, that they use under license from the original author.

Colophon

This book was prepared digitally using Open Source software. Writing and page layout were performed with OpenOffice.org running on Debian GNU/Linux and Ubuntu Linux. Images were prepared with GIMP.

OpenOffice.org:	www.openoffice.org
Debian GNU/Linux:	www.debian.org
Ubuntu Linux:	www.ubuntu.org
GIMP:	www.gimp.org

Version: 20070815

www.ingramcontent.com/pod-product-compliance
Lightning Source LLC
LaVergne TN
LVHW042334060326
832902LV00006B/165